From Hell and Back:

Survive and Thrive

To Betty + Ray
with Love
Gussie

A Life Story

of

Hope

Recovery and Success

First Edition

Design by Werner Graphic Design

Layout by Alicia Katz Pollock

Library of Congress 2008904398

Printed in the United States of America

By

United Graphics, Mattoon, IL

Dedication

To my mother, Della—she hated me. To my father, Lester—he loved me. To my brother, Dean, and my sister, Marjory—I thank them for protecting me from my mother. Each of us, in our own way, worked to end the hellish era of denial, shame, blame, and anger that plagued the Augustus family for too long. As we accepted and forgave ourselves, we accepted and forgave each other, and went forward in love and peace.

To my schoolteachers—they provided me with a safe haven where hitting wasn't allowed. Their acceptance and support gave me confidence in myself as a human being, They taught me to work toward success and not worry about defeat or failure because they are only temporary conditions. These wonderful human beings also stressed the importance of being honest and straightforward which explains my reputation for "saying it like it is." They gave me hope for the future.

To my wonderful husband, Chet McRobert, who rescued me, loved me unconditionally, and helped heal my wounded psyche. I owe him my life and I will love him forever.

Contents

Acknowledgements

Elizabeth Zack: BOOKCRAFTERS LLC, Editor

Jerry Werner: Werner Graphics, Artwork

Alicia Katz Pollock, RoyalWise Solutions, Layout

My Family

Marc—Donna—Skip—*Brad—Rita—Heather*

Greg—Kristina—Kindel—Tim

Family—Friends—Colleagues

Jill Arnel—Dean Augustus— Louise Augustus

Kate Brown—Orville Berger—Alene Bickel—Joseph Bizen

Kathy Bowman—Tina Carlson—Melanie Fallis—Bill Fallis

Gordon Cox—George Grijalva—Eula Grijalva—Joyce Lakey

Michael McKeever——Nancy Osa——Rodney Park

Bob Lakey—John Leuthauser— Linda Malone

Linda Usher—David Widmark—Sherrill Widmark

Chris Vaeretti —Howard Vacrettii—Bess Wills

Bradley Communications

Introduction

To be able to understand and eventually forgive my mother for trying to kill me when I was an infant, and for the violence I suffered at her hand as a child, I had to understand the source of her fury.

When Mother was dying at age seventy-nine, she told me that because she was the oldest daughter in her family, her father denied her a high school education and sentenced her to nineteen years of enslavement as the DeVoss household slave—from age fourteen to age thirty-three.

Mother had a reservoir of rage filled to overflowing because of the change of status in her life. She wasn't allowed to be angry over the injustice of her situation as a child and young woman, but it was safe for her to humiliate and brutalize her daughters.

Enslavement was the destiny of first-born girls in America. Women and children were chattel—the legal property of their fathers and husbands. They had the same legal status as the livestock in the barn—they could be beaten and slaughtered as a legal right of ownership.

After crossing the Atlantic Ocean to gain freedom and a better life in the Americas, British colonists adopted English Common Law including its definition of marriage. According to the Blackstone Commentaries, "The very being and legal existence of the woman is suspended during the marriage."

Abigail Adams urged her husband, John, to "Remember the Ladies and be more generous and favorable to them than your ancestors," as he left to attend the Constitutional Congress in 1776. Despite Abigail's pleas, civil rights for specific groups of people couldn't compete with the urgency to win the Revolutionary War.

After the colonists won the Revolutionary War, Abigail didn't fare any better even though John was then President. She cautioned her husband, "Do not put such unlimited power into the hands of the husbands. Remember all men would be tyrants if they could." John answered, "...I cannot but laugh. Depend on it, we know better than to repeal our *masculine system.*"

John Adams was right. Nothing changed when the thirteen British colonies became states united in a new federal constitutional republic—the United States of America. Married women remained non-persons with absolutely no legal rights. Individual states eased some restrictions, but the degree of limitation varied from state to state. This was the reality of married women's lives for more than two centuries.

The authors of the U.S. Constitution and the Bill of Rights didn't address the status of women head-on. They backed into keeping women non-persons without legal standing by addressing the rights of generic "people." The Constitution addressed the rights and responsibilities of "people, person, persons, electors, and citizens." The President was referred to then and still is today as "he and his." Amendment V in the Bill of Rights guaranteed various rights of "persons," and clarified the importance of gender by declaring that people, persons, electors and citizens could not be compelled to be a witness against "*him*self."

The generic language in the Constitution and Bill of Rights determined women's role as human beings. There is no doubt about how the lack of clarity affected their everyday lives. Marriage in the United States of America—the land of the free—was a mandatory merger and acquisition by the husband of all personal property owned by his wife prior to the wedding ceremony. State law appointed husbands as CEO's of the new conglomerate and only he could manage any property that formerly belonged to his wife.

Women were *chattel*—the property of their fathers and husbands. Their lives met every description of a slave as defined in *Webster's Merri*am *Collegiate Dictionary:* "Slave: One that is completely subservient to a dominating influence." "Slavery: The state of a person who is a chattel of another." "Chattel: the property of another."

In 1866, Congress passed the Fourteenth Amendment to the Constitution defining "citizens" and "voters" as *male*. No hedging—it was out in the open! Within two years, the Fourteenth Amendment was ratified by all the states.

One hundred ninety-five years after John Adams told Abigail, "Men will never give up the "masculine system," the Supreme Court ruling in Reed v. Reed finally classified women as "persons." Sally Reed had the audacity to think *she should have the right to be the executor of her teenage son Richard's estate instead of her philandering husband, Cecil, from whom she was divorced.* Sixteen Idaho lawyers refused to take Sally Reed's case, but finally Allen Derr signed on to challenge the system that limited women's legal status. Her husband then filed a lawsuit countering that only men had the right to be the executor of an estate—and the Idaho Supreme Court ruled in his favor.

In 1971, the U.S. Supreme Court overturned the Idaho Supreme Court decision with a ruling that Idaho laws violated the federal Equal Protection Clause in the Constitution. While Sally Reed was granted the right to be executor of her son's estate, the ruling did not send a strong and clearly defined message to State Courts that gender laws based on inequality were illegal.

In 1981, the Supreme Court continued its piecemeal approach to clarifying women's legal status by ruling against the few states that had still had Head and Master laws' that gave men unilateral control over property owned jointly with their wives.

4

In 1996, 220 years after Abigail Adams made her case for equality, the U.S. Supreme Court ruled that women were equal to men under the law. *The Ladies were finally remembered.*

Abigail Adams

John Adams

Legal Information Institute

United States Constitution
Bill of Rights— Amendment V

No **PERSON** shall be held to answer for a capital, or otherwise Infamous crime, unless on a presentment or indictment of a grand jury except in cases arising in the land or naval forces, or in the militia, when in actual service in time of war or public danger; nor shall any **PERSON** be subject for the same offense to be twice put in jeopardy of life or limb; nor shall be compelled in any criminal case to be a witness against **HIMSELF**, nor be deprived of life, liberty, or property, without due process of law; nor shall private property be taken for public use, without just compensation.

CHAPTER ONE

FROM FALLING TO FLYING

*I*t took decades for me to conquer my nightly terror.

The room was always dark and eerily quiet. Then I fell—down, down, down. With my arms reaching out and slightly bent upward, I looked up as I dropped through the darkness. Though calm during the fall, I awoke terrified, and with a jolt.

That nightly haunting first appeared when I was fourteen and it was my signature nightmare for thirty-one years. I thought it was just a dream. I did not connect the falls to the relationship with my mother, or to my fear of standing or being seated near the outside wall of high buildings.

My father was my mother's dead husband's brother. I was born more than nine months after her husband, Elmer Augustus, was struck by lightning and killed. That morning, she cooked her husband's breakfast, kissed him good-bye, and because he was a healthy young man, she expected to serve him dinner that night. He never returned.

I've tried to put myself in my mother's place and feel her desperation. Elmer had rescued her from slavery and she loved him. He was the father of her two children. He made a comfortable living, and she must have been terrified when she thought about how she would support two children, much less three, without his income.

As if that wasn't enough to worry about, more than half of Della's family shunned her because of my untimely birth. That gave her one more reason to hate me—the cause of all her problems.

I doubt her hatred of me arose from post-partum depression—a condition not yet discovered when I was born. However, if Della had been a victim of that hormonal imbalance, eventually she would have recovered, and then her attitude toward me would have changed from the angry *"If it wasn't for you...."* Still, how could she not have been somewhat depressed at the time? Her husband had been healthy and alive, and suddenly he was taken from her in a violent, unexpected death.

Della's desperate solution was to kill me, her unwanted daughter. My death had to be seen as *accidental* because infanticide was illegal. Women were seldom arrested for killing an infant. However, if they were caught, tried by a court and found guilty, they were sentenced to death by hanging.

With two teenagers coming and going, Della needed a plan. The murder would have to occur when she was alone in the house with me. Our house was large, but not quite a mansion. It was an impressive two-story shingled house with white-painted window trim. My sister, Marjory, told me that the kitchen was outfitted with a wood stove and a warming oven, as well as an oven for baking bread and cakes, and roasting succulent chickens and beef roasts. It had a wooden icebox with a block of ice in the bottom to keep food from spoiling. The counters were made of wood, and so was the table where the family gathered for meals.

In our kitchen, the counters stood higher than the table, so they would be ideal to stage an "accidental" death of her unwanted girl child. Because there was no crib, Mother would have had to pick me up from a bed or couch, and carry me through the house to the kitchen.

Then, according to Marjory, she propped me up on my side on the kitchen counter, and used a pillow to add momentum to the fall that she hoped would kill me.

I don't know how many times she acted on her mission of death. Was it only once, or was it several times until either Dean or Marjory caught her in the desperate and unthinkable act of trying to murder her infant daughter? This scenario buried itself in my unconscious memory, and came out of its hiding place to torture me night after night in my terror-filled dream of falling into the bottomless darkness. It didn't include my desperate mother.

I didn't question the reason for the nightmare for years. The dream was just part of my life. My sister, Marjory, finally helped me begin to resolve my nightly terror when I was forty-one. She had the missing piece to complete my psychic puzzle— the shocking news that when I was an infant my mother attempted to murder me. Marjory also told me they did interrupt her murder attempts, and took turns staying home from school to protect me.

Now that I know the reality of the dreams—it isn't pleasant to think about the details of my mother's murder attempts. However, I do have several questions, starting with: *Did they hurt?* Well-known psychologist and author David Chamberlain, Ph.D., Director of he Natural Child Project, notes, "Research at John Hopkins University in 1917 and at Washington University School of Medicine in St. Louis in the 1970s proved unequivocally that infants can feel pain." So the answer to my first question is, "Yes, I would have felt the pain of falling from the counter to the floor."

Did Mother ever wonder about the pain caused by her failed murder attempts? Probably not, is my guess: "If death is your goal, you probably aren't worried about the pain associated with your actions."

At the time, could I distinguish my mother's face from Marjory's? According to Dr. Chamberlain's Cesarean Voices Website, "studies show that newborn babies quickly learn to distinguish their mother's face from other female faces." "Yes, I could recognize the person causing my pain."

Could I anticipate her deadly actions? Studies by Colyn Trevarthen, Professor of Psychobiology at the University of Edinburgh, and Dr. Vasudevi Reddi, head of the University of Portsmouth Psychology Department, and their studies of other research lead me to believe the answer is yes: "Experiments show that a baby a few months old can connect experiences lived at different times." As a mother myself, I distinctly remember my two-month-old infant son's hungry cries stopping abruptly when he heard my footsteps approaching his room. "Yes, it seems reasonable that I could have anticipated pain when Mother approached me or held me."

Would I have been afraid at the sight of my mother at times when she wasn't trying to kill me? Dr. David Chamberlain reports on his Natural Child Project Website, "A new appreciation has emerged for the special characteristics of trauma-based memories." It seems reasonable to believe that memory is based on experience, so the answer is likely, "Yes, I would have experienced fear at the very sight of my mother."

Trevarthen and Reddi report, "A full term infant can track the sound of a mother's voice," so combined with their findings that infants can remember past experiences my answer is again, "Yes, as a helpless infant I could anticipate being hurt, but all I could have done was scream in fear." I couldn't run away as I did at age three when I packed my clothes in a cracker box and took off down the road, only to be herded back by our German Shepherd dog.

Why didn't the falling dreams begin earlier than age fourteen? Again, according to Dr. Chamberlain, "Trauma-based memories can be buried and repressed for long periods of time before being triggered by an event and admitted to consciousness." I believe there were three trigger events that gave the falls access to my dreams at age fourteen: 1) My father was sent to a tuberculosis sanatorium hundreds of miles away in The Dalles, a town located on the Columbia River; 2) My beloved sister, Marjory, moved even further away to California; and 3) My brother, Dean, was seriously injured in a logging accident that severed his spinal cord and paralyzed him from his waist to his feet.

I lost the three people in this world I could count on for love, support, and protection. I loved my father. His alcoholism made him unreliable, but he encouraged me to succeed and made it clear that he cared about me. Mother never hit me when my father was home. I loved my sister. and I loved my brother. Mother didn't hit me when they were around.

Even though I understood the rational reasons for these monumental changes in my life, I felt abandoned by everyone—left alone with my mother who hated me. I sank into total despair. I had giant hives, even on the bottom of my feet so I couldn't get away from my mother's furious attacks, and I started allergy shots.

What I remember most about that terrible year was the debut of my first nightly dream of plummeting down, down, down through the darkness. With my psychic guard damaged from the three trigger events, my mother's murder attempts gained access to my dreams, and they were the main stage attraction every night for thirty-one terrifying years.

Was my fear of being near the outside wall of high buildings in offices or restaurants related to the falls I experienced as an infant? Dr. Chamberlain discovered through his work that "hidden memories walk around disguised as fears." After I forced the memories of my mother's kitchen counter atrocities out of their dark hiding places, my fear of falling from the edge of anything high changed to flying with total confidence in myself and the world around me.

Three years after my sister told me about my mother's failed murder attempts, I had the opportunity and the determination to finally confront and conquer my fear of being near the edge of high buildings. My husband, Chet, was a Ford dealer, and we attended Ford Motor Company's 75th Anniversary Celebration in Detroit, Michigan. We stayed at the brand new seventy-three-story Renaissance Center Hotel. The lobby escalators hung in midair: They seemed to be suspended without any visible physical support. The glass elevator to the River Café seemed like any other elevator until it reached the third floor. Then, it suddenly shot up and out of the enclosed elevator shaft and clung to the outside walls on its upward climb to the top of the seventy-three-story-high Renaissance Center Tower.

The view of the Detroit River and Windsor, Canada must have been a wondrous sight from the Tower's glass elevator. I wouldn't know. What I do know is it was not a good place to be if you had any fear of falling off the edge of high buildings.

At the time, though, I thought to myself, *"This is ridiculous! Enough already."* Determined to conquer my fear, I told Chet I was going to skip the meetings and face my demons on the treacherous edges of the free-hanging escalator and the sky-high glass elevator clinging to the outside of the Renaissance Center. Chet understood since he had seen the terrified look on my face when we were trapped in the back of that glass elevator.

He wasn't the only one who saw a woman frozen in fear in that elevator. A man who had held the door open for everyone to leave the elevator was waiting for his wife to exit when he took one look at me, put his arm in front of her, and said, "We'd better let that woman out of here." I took him up on his offer.

The next day, and every day until the 75th Anniversary Celebration ended, I rode the suspended escalators and the clinging-to-the-outside glass elevator in sheer terror, over and over, until my fear completely disappeared. Being free of fear was my own 31st Anniversary Celebration!

Each repetition reprogrammed my wounded psyche, neutralized my mother's murder attempts, and ended my nightly terror. My dreams changed overnight to adventures: flying over green fields and forests, and soaring over mountaintops like a falcon—swooping and climbing and diving. I look forward to these nightly adventures—they are absolutely amazing.

1. Renaissance Center, Detroit, Michigan. 2. Marjory and Dean Augustus
3. Doris DeVoss Whitney 4. Duane Whitney, Norma Augustus, Bill Whitney.

CHAPTER TWO
FAMILY SECRETS & THE BLACK SHEEP

The Kansas State Constitution approved in 1861, guaranteed women equal privileges with men in the ownership of property and control of children. The Constitution also guaranteed tax-supported public education for all children. It did not, however, guarantee women and children equality as persons with legal status and standing in the courts. Nor did it promise protection of women and children from the tyranny of societies unwritten expectations.

The destiny of my mother, Della DeVoss, was predetermined by the widely held practice and expectation that as the oldest daughter in the family, she would serve as her family's "second" mother caring for the household and her younger brothers and sisters.

It was not optional. Della had no choice because she was her parents' property and they had the right to enslave her without any regard for her feelings or how it would affect her future. The authors of the Kansas Constitution "supported public education," but they did not mandate school attendance. They were also silent about gender and age.

Although the Kansas Constitution gave her mother, Carolyn, the legal right to be involved in the "control of children," Della was uncertain whether her mother participated in the discussions that led to the final decision. She told me it was her father, Edward, who told her that her school days were over at age fourteen. She was the only one who was not allowed to attend high school—her seven brothers and sisters all graduated from high school so it wasn't that he thought female children should not get an education.

Della "had to help her mother" with the increasing workload as child after child joined the family. Under the Comstock Law, even having information about birth control was a federal crime. Birth control devices such as condoms and diaphragms were available by the 1860s, but expensive. Mother said this subject was never discussed openly in the DeVoss household.

As the industrial revolution flourished, the need for workers increased and support for limiting family size decreased. President Theodore Roosevelt declared birth control was "decadent and a sign of moral disease." The Comstock Law, approved by Congress in 1879, was not overturned until 1965 when the Supreme Court ruled it was unconstitutional in Griswold v. Connecticut.

To Edward and Carolyn, their oldest daughter was simply extra household help. They sentenced her to be their household slave for an undetermined number of years. It turned out to be a nineteen year sentence that began when she was fourteen—and ended when she was thirty-three.

Della was a good student, so her enslavement made it even harder for her to accept her limited role as a housemaid. Her life was to be day after day of domestic drudgery. This was not just the oldest daughter helping out—taking care of the family consumed her entire young life. Poverty was not the reason her father enslaved Della. Edward and his wife Carolyn were able, for example, to pay college tuition for another daughter, Doris.

Della's restricted life as the oldest daughter was the same as oldest daughters across America. Their non-negotiable role as white slaves is confirmed by every definition of slavery found in the Merriam-Webster's Collegiate Dictionary. *Slave: One that is completely subservient to a dominating influence. Slavery: The state of a person who is a chattel of another. Chattel: Property.*

Della's immediate and extended family and the community in which she lived accepted Della's slave status without question. She was trapped with no escape and no place to hide.

You can see and feel the hopelessness she felt in photographs taken when she was a young woman. Her eyes have a hollow look. She was attractive and the home-sewn dresses she made were stylish, not just sacks that hung on her. But there is never even a hint of a smile on her face in any of the photographs.

Her father was her slave master for eighteen years, and her grandfather for one year. Their power over her was absolute. Women were expected to be submissive to men and do exactly what they were told without questioning male authority. It wouldn't have been any different for a fourteen-year old girl who, like the cows in the barn, was the property of her father.

Della must have wondered what they would do to her if she didn't obey. But she didn't dare challenge the authority of her father and grandfather. Male domination was the foundation on which all male/female relationships were based. Husbands and fathers could beat women and children as a legal right of ownership. Fathers could abandon children in orphanages if they weren't obedient or give them away to another family. Fear was the safety mechanism that kept Della in line.

While Della had to comply, she didn't have to like it. How could she not be angry about the injustice of it all? Her life changed from that of a carefree schoolgirl to a woman responsible for the care and feeding of her sisters and brothers, the housework, and more. It must have been her anger that fed her soul and kept her going—day after day after day for nineteen terrible years. She was absolutely furious and the seething, fuming ball of fire in her chest contaminated her personal relationships for decades.

Della's family model learned from her parents was the *norm* for the time. Daughters were just worthless girls who could do nothing right, and by virtue of their gender, a son was highly valllued as an asset to the family and could do no wrong.

Thinking about the rigid control and the tyranny she endured for almost twenty years brings tears to my eyes even today. I simply cannot imagine surviving nineteen years of slavery.

Della's father did not handle the situation with caring and gratitude for what Della would have to give up in order to help their expanding family. Edward specifically and the DeVoss family in general never addressed the unfairness and inequities caused by the almost twenty-year enslavement that robbed Della of an education, social skills, career possibilities, and the self-esteem that went along with the

Could her sisters Carolyn, Louise, and Doris have taken turns helping Della out? Well, the answer today is obvious—Yes. But Edward didn't look to Carolyn, Louise, or Doris to help run the household because they were above Della in status and standing in the family. To her father, Della was no different than the livestock he pastured and slaughtered. She was a commodity to be used for his benefit. When the Supreme Court ruled that women were "persons" with legal standing in 1971, it was much too late to help Della who was then seventy-six years old.

Of Della's four brothers: the twins, George and Walter, and Leonard and Lloyd—only one, Lloyd, the youngest brother, led a "normal" life. He worked, married and raised a son. He also served in the Army in World War II. Leonard married, had two daughters, divorced, and thereafter spent time in a mental hospital, working when he could at menial jobs. His immediate family blames the De Voss family for all of his shortcomings.

The twins, George and Walter, served in the Army in World War II, but spent the rest of their lives wandering from state to state working at whatever odd jobs they could find. In their later years they stayed mostly in Nevada. Being put on a pedestal, pampered, and spoiled rotten as boys apparently didn't give them the life skills they needed as men.

The women in the DeVoss family fared better than the men. Their lives were more stable. Carolyn and Louise had high school educations, married and raised families. Doris married, had two sons, and later divorced her husband. With her college degree, she was able to teach in public schools in California. She stands out as the only sister who kept in touch with Della after her banishment, regularly corresponding with her over the years.

Della's hours, like her mother Carolyn's, were determined by the work that had to be done. Raising seven children is time consuming even today, but in the early 1900s with no electricity everything had to be done tediously by hand.

Lighting the house at night in the late 1800s and early 1900s meant candles if rural families couldn't afford the glass lamps or tin lanterns and the various fluids to light them ranging from whale oil, turpentine, to kerosene distilled from coal. Since the DeVoss family could afford them, Della spent her evenings close to the lamps doing hand sewing, and reading her brother's and sister's school books when she had time.

The DeVoss farm was in northeastern Kansas. Marshall County was one of the original counties when the State was founded in 1861. The closest town was Waterville, established in 1867, on the Little Blue River at the end of a railroad line. It was a thriving business center for the rural farming community with hardware and grocery stores, a post office, bank, hotel, church, school, and an opera house. I always assumed that the town was named Waterville because of its close proximity to the river, but the name was the doing of William Osborne, a railroad superintendent who wanted to perpetuate the name of his hometown, Waterville, New York.

In the late 1800s, there was one portable house in Waterville where railroad workers lived temporarily until the rail lines were completed. Newcomers lived in tents. Today, Waterville's population is 681 people, with 190 families living in 328 homes. Many are century houses built of stone. Waterville may still be small, but it is just as prosperous as it was a century ago.

According to Orville Berger, who owned a farm near Waterville in the early 20th century, the farms in the Edward DeVoss era in the late 1800s and early 1900s were diversified with pastureland for livestock and crops including oats, corn, wheat, milo for sorghum, and alfalfa. It was the Waterville feed lot, the supply center for the area, and the railroad line that ended there that made it possible for farmers to have additional income. The rail line is now a tourist attraction.

The DeVoss family would have enjoyed the amenities available in Waterville today: community theatre productions, two museums, a community center, a public swimming pool, and lighted tennis courts and ball fields. Their only recreational outings would have been limited to attending the opera or church and school events, and in the summer picnics and swimming in Lake Idlewild, located one mile north of town.

The Thomas home was the first Waterville house updated to end the burdensome job of carrying buckets filled with water drawn from a well. It had a cistern on a hill behind the house, and since water flows downhill there was adequate water pressure to equip the home with running water. Out on the flatland DeVoss farm, however, Della had to pull water up and out of a well in buckets. A central pump outside was a big improvement years later, but it still meant water had to be carried to wherever it was needed.

Orville Berger says it wasn't until September 1941 when President Franklin D. Roosevelt's Rural Electrification Agency (REA) brought electricity to Waterville. It was a new day for Waterville farm families, but too late for Della since she moved to Colorado in 1914. The new fangled innovation must have improved her mother Carolyn's life. With electricity the DeVoss family could then pump water from cisterns or springs and wells into the house, and stop carrying bucket after bucket filled to the brim with water as they had done for years.

They used metal washboards for laundry until they were replaced by electric automatic washing machines. Orville Berger said the fancy new electric machines increased the need for more water, which meant building more cisterns and searching for additional springs. Electricity also simplified the men's lives. Water troughs were electrified and didn't freeze in the winter, so it was no longer necessary to chip ice to make room for the water hand-carried in buckets for the cattle and horses.

Because electricity had not yet reached Waterville, when Della was a fourteen-year old child who had to do the family laundry, her day began with carrying pail after pail of water from the outdoor pump to the kitchen. Then she had to heat the water in a wash boiler or tub on the stove, and when it was steaming hot she scrubbed the soiled clothes on the washboard—back and forth until they were clean. Rinsing the clean clothes in a tub meant Della had to carry more buckets filled with water from the pump outside. Finally she would wring out the clean, rinsed clothes by hand, then hang them up to dry on clotheslines outside. She completed her laundry task only after ironing the items with an iron heated on a wood stove. Doesn't it make you tired just thinking about having to do that whole routine every week?

Della also had to help clean and care for her mother's seven younger children.

One tub, filled not quite to the brim with water carried in buckets and heated on the wood-stove, washed several family members. Other chores included gardening—growing and harvesting enough fresh vegetables to sustain the household. Then the house had to be cleaned, and meals cooked on the wood-stove, which meant wood had to be chopped and carried to the kitchen. In her spare time, Della would sew and mend clothing by hand, or later on a sewing machine powered by pumping pedals with her feet.

Della's life was chore after chore after chore for six-days a week. On Sunday they rested—kind of.

Even with two full-time workers, a woman and a child, the DeVoss family responsibilities with eight children were daunting. Although Mother never talked about her mother, Carolyn, the feeling I have about their relationship is that while they were in a difficult situation, they were a team. They would have had to work together to survive the absolutely backbreaking days they put in. Della's help was clearly needed, but it was the mean spirited way in which her father went about enslaving her that caused Della so much misery. He never treated her with the respect she deserved.

After she had a stroke, my husband, Chet, and I had to close her duplex home. We found some old family photographs in her trunk. One was particularly troubling. It was a large group of people standing on risers looking very serious and formal. I was stunned when I saw the agonized look on my mother's face. I asked her why she looked so sad. Mother explained that the extended family had "gathered to say goodbye to her mother, father, and brothers and sisters" because they were moving to Montana. She was the only family member not included in the move. Della was her father's gift to her grandfather. She was just a servant with a new assignment. She was a throwaway daughter.

Facing death at age seventy-nine must have given Mother the courage to remember and talk about her childhood trials as the oldest daughter and her enslavement. It was a chilling story. I wondered why her parents weren't punished because none of my history classes, even in the gender-neutral progressive high school I attended, included women as chattel—the legal property of men.

Della didn't have much to say about her grandfather, Isaac DeVoss, other than he was a Methodist minister who controlled every aspect of life in her parent's home. Reverend DeVoss prohibited all music, dancing, and games. Emotions were forbidden as ungodly and his iron-fisted religious rules were never questioned.

From Saturday at sundown to Monday at sunrise, their activities were limited to Bible readings, attending church, and eating cold food because cooking was forbidden. It was a day off, but not particularly restful or relaxing.

Any protest by Della about being left behind to serve her grandparents would have been severely punished. It would have been time for the belt. But her facial expression in the photo documented her pain and sense of betrayal.

Della had no choice except to do the backbreaking work assigned to her day after day until she married Elmer Augustus in 1914. Mother said, "It was an act of God." She told me they moved to Blanca, Colorado because the Kansas ragweed caused her asthma. It was also a way to escape the daily reminders of her years as the DeVoss household slave. It was a fresh start with a new life in a new place.

Elmer was an important man in the community. He worked as a "ditch rider" and was responsible for keeping the irrigation canals in good repair to provide water for crops in arid southern Colorado. They had two children, Marjory and Dean.

Unfortunately, Elmer was struck by lightning and killed while he was riding the irrigation ditches looking for holes and any weaknesses in the dikes. Marjory was sixteen. Dean was eighteen.

Since most of the Augustus family lived in Kansas, the funeral for Elmer was held in Waterville instead of their home in Blanca, Colorado. When the grieving Augustus family gathered for Elmer's funeral, they were surprised to see Lester, the oldest brother and family outcast at the ceremony. But Lester wanted to honor his brother since he had no hard feelings against his mother or his brothers and sisters. His stepfather, Frank, was the only Augustus that he never wanted to see again.

In an era when sexual relationships between unmarried men and women were forbidden, and without any regard for the possible consequences, Lester struck up a relationship with the grieving widow. Della was devastated by Elmer's death and Lester probably took advantage of her vulnerability. The price she paid for her secret sexual trysts was an illegitimate daughter.

To say she was not overjoyed by my untimely birth—more than nine months after her husband was killed—is quite an understatement.

Did it even occur to her to say no to my father's sexual advances? Mother's childhood indoctrination was the norm for the time: When men said, "Jump!" the only question a woman could ask was, "How high?" Was Mother a willing partner but regretted the outcome? Was there real attraction? Or were finances a bigger concern—without Elmer's income, and with her limited education, could she support her family without a husband? They are all legitimate concerns and probably influenced her response to Lester.

Della's grandfather, Reverend Isaac DeVoss, used his religious authority to condemn Della's indiscretion. His rejection edict went out to the entire DeVoss family and the Waterville, Kansas church community. Della was more than an embarrassment to her extended family. She was a disgrace.

What was the day-to-day effect of her grandfather's banishment on Della's life? At the time, Della lived in Blanca, Colorado, and the Isaac DeVoss clan was based in Kansas, so his anger may not have affected her community directly unless the Waterville church had ties in Blanca. The DeVoss family had been trained from the cradle that they had to obey the Reverend's orders, even if it was an edict to banish his granddaughter for her sexual indiscretion.

The question for the Reverend, his wife, the seven DeVoss siblings, and their mother and father was whether to banish and shun their sister, daughter, and granddaughter or forgive her error in judgment for getting pregnant without a husband. The score at the end of that sorry vote was eight in favor of banishing Della and three against. Only one sister, Doris, and two brothers, Leonard and Lloyd disobeyed Reverend DeVoss. It was a landslide victory for the preacher.

These were the same parents who enslaved Della for nineteen years and the very brothers and sisters that Della, as the oldest daughter household slave, had nurtured from birth. She had changed their diapers, concocted herbal plasters and mixtures to cure whatever bug was going around, did their laundry, and cooked their meals while they were off having a merry time at school. Della paid a high price for being their servant and most of the ingrates didn't have the courage to stand up for her. Instead, they caved in to their grandfather's wishes to kick her while she was down.

I have no memories as a youngster of ever seeing my grandparents or the four sibling cowards who banished my mother because she gave birth to an illegitimate daughter, with the exception of a VERY brief visit by two of the "Banish her!" voters, George and Walter. They showed up at our house once making it clear they wanted long-term free room and board; my father made them leave after a couple of days. It was obvious they wanted the oldest-sister-caregiver relationship they had known as children instead of a visit with their sister.

I vaguely remember one cross-country trip in our Ford panel truck, but where we went or the people we visited comes up blank. Two of the brave brothers, Lloyd and Leonard, moved to Oregon and lived nearby. The only sister with gumption enough to stand up to the Reverend was Doris. She and Della corresponded by mail and later with telephones they could actually talk to each other. Doris visited us once in Klamath Falls, and after Della died, she came to Gresham to visit my family.

Many years later, however, the DeVoss family had the nerve to send the father of their clan to Oregon. They wanted Della to take care of him when he became senile and ill. My one memory of him is that I was the only one who could convince the old coot to take a bath. Della finally stood up to them. As his health deteriorated she sent her father, Edward, the man who rejected her when I was born, back to her ungrateful brothers and sisters. Good riddance!

Completing the story about Della's fall from grace has to include the Frank Augustus family. Her father-in law, Frank, would have been outraged at what he would have perceived as disloyalty to his son Elmer, her deceased husband. In addition to her disloyalty to Elmer, her choice to have a sexual relationship with Lester, who Frank hated, rubbed salt on his own festering and very open wounds because Lester was the illegitimate son of his wife, Ida. Della couldn't have chosen anyone more likely to cause outrage and rejection from Frank Augustus than his stepson Lester.

The Augustus family would eventually have the last word on this event. Their disdain for Lester spread to his brother Elmer's children, Dean and Marjory. Was it because they kept the source of the Augustus family embarrassment alive? If Mother's murder attempts had succeeded, my birth could have been swept under the carpet with the rest of the Augustus dirt. Instead, every day I lived reminded Frank that he was not the first man to have sexual relations with his wife, Ida. Frank then waited a lifetime to get even with anyone named Augustus who was related to Lester. I hope Frank Augustus is rotting in whatever hell he created for himself.

I was eighteen when my very quiet and dignified Aunt Anna Augustus, the widow of Lester's brother, Harry, told me that Lester's father was not Frank Augustus. It was a difficult story for her to tell—the embarrassment of such goings on in their family! I took her cue and didn't ask for details. Lester's birth status was our first family secret.

The information about Lester's birth father, although late in coming, helped me understand my father. It was not something that my father ever discussed with us as a family. I would like to have had the opportunity to tell him that his birth status didn't affect my love for him.

The McMillan story was revealed to me gradually over half a century—from 1952 to 1998. During my psychiatric nursing rotation at the State Mental Hospital in Salem, Oregon, some fifty miles south of Portland, I became acquainted with my cousin, Doris Derthick, who lived there.

In 1998, when I was clarifying information about my grandmother, Ida Augustus, for a family history I was writing, I asked Doris for specifics. She told me that "A Mr. McMillan" was my grandfather, not Frank Augustus. She didn't know Mr. McMillan's first name but she said he was a wealthy business tycoon and that he had generously provided for Ida and Lester. Doris acknowledged that with that detail, I finally knew the whole story about my father's birth status. It was our first family secret to be pulled out of the darkness to die in the sunshine. The extended Augustus family could no longer pretend my father was an unimportant member of their family. If I had confronted them with the facts of Mr. McMillan's generosity, they would have had to acknowledge that Lester's birth was the only reason for the financial wealth they all enjoyed.

Lester was the only Augustus sibling who wasn't diabetic. The McMillan blood flowing in Lester's veins must have protected him—he escaped the Augustus plague.

Mr. McMillan was an honorable man and he felt responsible for the future of Ida, and their son, Lester. He arranged for her to marry Frank Augustus and bought them a mansion and a substantial farm in Vermillion, Kansas. I always thought the farm was in Waterville, but handwriting on a photograph names the location as Vermillion.

The average Kansas farmer could not afford such an impressive house: two-and-a-half stories high with sleeping quarters in what amounted to a third floor. There was a second floor balcony and a covered porch on the first floor leading to the front door. The house was painted a neutral beige color and was highlighted with white painted trim outlining the structure as well as the windows. The yard was beautifully landscaped with formal gardens and a long twisting, curving path that made its way to the front door. It was a magnificent farmhouse and it demonstrated Mr. McMillan's generosity to Ida and Lester.

Frank never adopted Lester. However, Lester was thought of as an Augustus and used his stepfather's last name as his own. He didn't have a middle name like his brothers and sisters. His mother and stepfather gave no reason for their inaction except that they "never got around to it." They accepted the farm that Mr. McMillan so generously gave them because of Lester's birth but they couldn't make the effort to give him a middle name. He signed his name, Lester A. Augustus giving himself at least an initial so he must have felt it was an affront not to have a middle name. Now I wonder why he chose A. for anonymous instead of M. for McMillan. Every time he signed his name was a reminder that his mother and stepfather thought him less worthy than his brothers and sisters.

The Augustus family wanted to forget the reason they lived in a big, fancy house and didn't have to worry about money— their mother gave birth to an illegitimate baby.

If my father knew about Mr. McMillan, his birth father and his generosity, he didn't talk about it at least when I was around. I feel that he did know the whole story because at least one brother, Harry, knew about the McMillan connection and he passed the Lester-McMillan legend down at least one generation to his daughter, Doris Derthick.

I remember Doris in 1952 casually mentioning looking forward to their annual $5000 check from the Augustus family. Now I wonder why I didn't connect the dots between her family and my family and ask why we didn't receive a similar payment. A $5000 check would have been welcomed at our house, too.

Mr. McMillan's generosity was a double-edged sword for Frank Augustus. Yes, the farm belonged to Frank Augustus, but he didn't earn it the old fashioned way. He knew everyone in the community was aware that he didn't inherit the farm from his parents and he didn't buy it with money he had earned. Frank's masculine status and reputation in the community were based on Mr. McMillan's success. Frank had been bought and paid for specifically to take care of Ida and Lester. Frank's brutal beatings violated his agreement with Mr. McMillan to care for his son, but who in the Augustus family would have dared report the violation and endanger their wealthy livelihood?

If Lester had been shy and retiring his life might have been easier. His stepfather used his fists and a belt to squelch Lester's confidant, happy-go-lucky, daredevil approach to life. Although the Kansas Constitution gave Ida legal rights equal to Frank's when it came to "controlling" or raising children, it's unlikely she would have interfered with Frank's harsh discipline and risk getting beaten herself.

Lester was alone in a family that resented him. Did Ida show Lester any affection at all as a mother? I believe there were some positive feelings between them because they're not stone-faced in the one photograph I have of them. There seems to be closeness between them. I hope for my father's sake that it's not just my wishful imagination and I would like to believe he had at least a few moments when he felt loved and wanted in the Augustus family.

Boys age five or six could do simple chores, so Lester could have helped feed the chickens and, by the age ten, done more complex work like gardening with supervision. As a teenager, Lester could easily have fed and watered the cattle and horses that roamed the pastureland as well as operate farm machinery. But his work never satisfied his critical stepfather no matter how hard he tried to please him, so the beatings continued.

Lester escaped his stepfather's abuse by running away from home at age sixteen. He must have visited his family occasionally because he was included I some family photographs. Lester's independence came at a high price. However, getting away from the absolutely hellish life he suffered under Frank's roof was not worth staying just to live in a mansion.

His first home after running away to escape from his brutal step-father was a sod-roofed stone house that he shared with some other young men. The surrounding fields grew mostly weeds but their garden produced a bumper crop of corn. The men worked on local farms doing whatever odd jobs they could find. I keep a photo on my desk that shows my father and three friends standing in front of their grass-roofed house. I think of it as a symbol of his freedom and courage to start a new life away from his abusive stepfather.

Lester thought he could make more money working in the lead mines, but he contracted lead poisoning from a hand injury. His life hung in the balance until doctors amputated the infected finger and he survived. He joked about his "stub" finger, and even though it was the first finger on his right hand, the deformity didn't handicap him in any way.

Despite the risks, Lester went back to work at the almost-lethal lead mine, saved his money and bought a trucking company. Lester loved the good times. He owned and raced greyhound dogs and horses, and he was introduced to moonshine whiskey. When federal agents came to town during Prohibition, it was Lester's trucks that moved the illegal stills that he and his friends used to make the prized moonshine.

Those same trucks also delivered a new miracle drug to the Augustus farm and Lester saved his brother's life. Guy was in a diabetic coma and dying, until the insulin arrived and miraculously saved his life. Someone in the family must have contacted Lester and asked for help. He could have refused, because nobody in the Augustus family ever came to his rescue when his stepfather was beating him. He treated them far better than he had ever been treated.

Did Frank ever thank Lester for saving Guy's life? I doubt that Frank had the manhood to get the words out of his mouth, because Lester would certainly have included such unexpected actions from his stepfather in that story which he told often. That was the caring and compassionate father I knew when he was sober.

The extended Augustus and DeVoss families always assumed that Lester was the father of Della's baby, Norma Jean Augustus. Did the townspeople know for certain who was Norma Jean's father? The timing of my birth and with Lester being the only man in Mother's life at that critical time, the answer is very likely a strong yes.

People used to say I looked just like my father, meaning Lester, particularly our widow's peak hairlines and facial features. There was no physical resemblance between me, my brother and sister, or my aunts and uncles on the DeVoss side of the family. Their facial structure was different than mine—wider and shorter. I was taller than Marjory by the time I was a teenager. My hair is thick and coarse, with a slight wave like my father's hair. I didn't pay any attention to Dean's hair, but unlike mine, Marjory's hair was extremely fine and she complained often about being limited to one hairstyle. Lester and I must resemble the McMillan side of his birth family. Even though my understanding that Lester was my father was upheld, I knew in some way, subconsciously before I was told, that it wasn't the whole story.

Della never accepted responsibility for her part in the sexual act that resulted in her pregnancy. Instead, she blamed me, her daughter, for the pregnancy that brought about her shameful fall from grace, and her unsatisfactory life in general. "If it wasn't for you…" was her angry accusation I heard every day. That' was one way she defused her violent hatred of me—and the fury that came with it. Another more violent defusing method was her beatings and floggings that started after we moved to Oregon.

I don't know if my father left Della's home and returned to Parker and his successful business after I was born. If he had been with us in Blanca, I feel strongly that he would have protected me.

Even if Dean and Marge were unsure about my father's willingness to protect me from our mother, they could not have prevented them from moving out of state. All I know for certain is when I was three years old, my brother, Dean and my sister, Marjory moved to Oregon; and Della, Lester, and Norma Jean Augustus headed for the Montana Rocky Mountains. Dean came to Montana once to visit, or was it to check on my safety?

My parents may have known about work in the Montana mining industry from the DeVoss family. Our arrival in Montana, however, coincided with the Basin Montana Tunnel Company's sale of certificates to finance a mining venture.

The news that there was a silver rush gave my father and mother an opportunity to start a new life where nobody knew about them, the Augustus or DeVoss families, or the birth status of the girl traveling with them.

Lester had wavy snow-white hair and stood tall and proud. Della's hair was grey but she kept it cut and styled with her own scissors and curling irons that she heated on the stove. They were an attractive couple, but time had taken a toll on both of them. They appeared to be too old to have a young daughter. In fact, I was asked more than a few times over the years if they were my grandparents, and also whether my parents been killed in an accident. The move away from the community where their relationship was common knowledge was the beginning of the Augustus Family Secret era.

"Basin" was the name my family called the mining camp where we lived. To me the name described the mountains that completely surrounded the camp. A circle of mountaintops formed a concave shaped crater wide enough and deep enough for a mining operation and housing for the miner's families. At the crater's bottom was a creek, shaded by willows, that ran free until it froze in the winter. The Basin Tunnel Company owned the mine and had offices in the nearby town of Basin, so the name didn't describe the shape of the crater that so impressed the young girl from flatland Colorado.

Basin was high in the Rocky Mountains near Boulder, a town halfway between Butte and Helena. The mountains, the trees, the blue sky—it was a beautiful setting. The houses that the miners and their families lived in were midway up the mountains. The mine's smelter and processing plants were in the lowest part of the crater, as were the old abandoned store fronts and the saloon with a stage—all ghost town reminders of boom-times in the past.

Lester was no longer a prosperous employer nor the owner of a trucking company. No more racehorses and greyhounds running around the track. The good times were gone except for the whiskey. It wasn't moonshine, but it was plentiful, and must have eased the pain of having to work in a silver mine deep in the ground. He never complained about the hard, gritty work.

Clearly, my birth had affected my father's life. Unlike my mother, my father did not blame me for the change in his circumstances. However, it had to be another raw spot added to those inflicted by his stepfather, Frank Augustus. Even the Rocky Mountains could not heal the damage.

Della and Lester were unhappy. They yelled at each other. He slapped Mother and she cried. I suspected the arguments and fights were caused by whatever it was my father drank from the brown bottles. His anger grew as he drank glass after glass of the mysterious liquid. I understood that my mother didn't want my father to leave the house when she tried to hide the car keys. More yelling. More hitting. The house was too small to have a hiding place for a frightened little girl so I was a witness to those events. I wondered if I was next in line, but my father never hit me.

Thirty-five years later, Mother confirmed a repressed memory I recalled during a Gestalt counseling session: I was in the dark, and I was shivering and very, very cold. I asked her if she had any thoughts about that revelation and why I always hated being cold. She told me that one frigid Montana winter night, my father left me in his Ford panel truck in downtown Boulder while he played poker and drank whiskey. He got in a drunken brawl with a deputy sheriff and hit him with a broken whiskey bottle. That cost him a night in jail.

Nobody knew that the drunken brawler's five-year old daughter sat alone in the dark in her father's black panel truck. A woman walking down the street noticed me, realized that something was wrong, and took me to her house to spend the night. The next morning, the nice woman took me to the sheriff's office. By then my sober father remembered that he had a daughter. We drove back to the mining camp in the black Ford panel truck as if nothing unusual had happened.

Did Mother try to prevent my father from taking me with him to drink and play poker? What was she thinking? She had to know that I'd either be in the saloon with the drunken gamblers or alone in the car, and that neither option was safe for a five-year old girl. Mother showed no emotion when she told me this horror story. It was just something that had happened. I would like to believe that she tried and failed to convince my father that it was a bad idea. As usual, I didn't ask her to explain. I was afraid she might answer, "I just didn't care."

My half-sister, Dorothy, who I saw only twice in my life, told me years later that Lester did the same thing to her and that was the reason her mother Dorothy, however, idealized her father as a romantic figure. Her daughter,

Colleen, called me in the late 1990s asking for his birth records because Dorothy had told her that Lester was half Native American Indian, and Colleen wanted to apply for benefits.

I assured Colleen that her grandfather was Swedish and maybe some German and/or Scottish. She didn't want to hear that he was an alcoholic and a rogue even if he was a lovable rogue. I left telephone messages about needing an address to send her photographs of her mother and grandfather, but she never returned my calls. Finally, I obtained her address from a friend and mailed them to her. She never acknowledged receiving the photos and the mining memorabilia that I sent. I saw my half-sister, Dorothy, for the last time when she came to our father's funeral.

We lived in Montana until I was seven and then we moved to southern Oregon to be near Dean and Marjory in Klamath Falls. Lester found work at the Kesterson lumber mill. He still drank, played poker, and lost the money we needed to survive. If there was any money left, he bought soybean futures. Wall Street provided his ultimate gambling fix. Our one-story rectangular house with composite brick siding was unfinished inside for years.

Working together in the garden was the only thing my parents did together without fighting. Lester argued with Della about everything—she couldn't do anything right. She would retaliate by reminding him that he did little that was good. He abused her physically. She took her anger out on me—I was her scapegoat. We were a classic alcoholic dysfunctional family and the hostile atmosphere poisoned my childhood. The only time Della wasn't picking me apart was when she needed my help with something—say, laundry, or canning and freezing vegetables and fruit.

Lester developed health problems. He lost weight and coughed incessantly. Doctors pulled his teeth and told him to stop drinking but he continued to lose weight. Finally, two years after Lester first sought help, doctors ordered a chest X–ray. That delay allowed the mycobacterium tuberculosis to spread throughout both lungs. When I was fourteen years old and in the eighth grade, Lester was sent to a tuberculosis sanatorium in The Dalles, Oregon, where doctors hoped that collapsing a lobe of one lung, bed rest, and the dry climate would cure his TB. The dry climate failed to cure his tuberculosis, and he died four years later.

I was a senior in high school and almost eighteen when he died. I had another attack of giant hives and my hair turned gray from the stress of losing the only one of my parents who loved me. I felt abandoned, but I had some wonderful memories of my father, Lester. He liked to garden and grow exotic vegetables from packages of seeds he ordered from catalogs. Kohlrabi was his favorite. He enjoyed camping, fishing, and training our dogs, Lady, a black Labrador, and Pudge, a golden Chesapeake, to hunt and do tricks. He took me pheasant and duck hunting. He was a champion checker player. He taught me to play checkers and to my mother's dismay, he also taught me to shoot craps. He gave me a dollar for every A on my report card. He was the only one who could explain mathematics to me and without his patient teaching my math grades plummeted.

I also have memories that bring back fear and trembling. He was an alcoholic. He made me cry. He made me laugh. Sometimes I hated him. Sometimes I loved him with all my heart.

I have made peace with my father, Lester A. Augustus. I am grateful for his unwavering support, his unconditional love, and his view of me as a person of value. He was scarred from his stepfather's brutality and being an unwanted child held in servitude from which he could not escape as a youngster. He did the best he could with the life skills he had at the time. That's all anyone can do.

Just before Lester died, his sister, Ethel, traveled to our home from Nyssa, a small town in eastern Oregon to tell us the family had decided to exclude Lester and his deceased brother Elmer's children, Dean and Marjory, from the Augustus estate. She gave no reason for the family's decision and we didn't ask. It smells like Frank, Sr. didn't want Mr. McMillan's son to have even one dollar from the estate that the Augustus family would not have inherited without Lester's birth and his father's generosity. The Augustus estate had to be substantial. The federal government paid the family a generous settlement when a newly-built dam covered the farm with water. It was enough to give $5,000 gifts every year to the children of the four Augustus brothers and one sister. In the 1950s, $5,000 was real money.

When Ethel asked us to pray with her before she left, Della not only showed her the door—she slammed it behind her. Money brings out the true nature in people. I wouldn't accept even once cent of the Augustus money if it arrived in the mail today. Over time there were two suicides in the family— Lester's brother and his nephew—so the McMillan/Augustus fortune didn't always bring happiness.

After Lester's death, Della faced the possibility of having a new and very different life than she had as an enslaved daughter and the common law wife of an alcoholic. Friends and neighbors stepped in to help and our family of two did quite well.

Our house, in farm country south of Klamath Falls, served as the neighborhood animal shelter and Della was known as the animal rescue woman. Neighbors brought her newly born lambs, calves, rabbits, puppies, and kittens: the runts of the litter too small to fend for themselves. Whether to make amends for trying to end one life or to experience the unconditional love that was absent from her life as a child, Della cared for them all. There was always a box by the stove and hot water bottles and blankets to keep them warm. We took turns getting up at night to feed them bottles of milk. It was safe for my mother to love and be loved by animals.

The same neighbors fixed the pump in our well so we would have water inside the house, helped with chores we couldn't manage, and gave us rides to town until my mother felt comfortable driving the black Ford panel truck. It was neighbors helping neighbors.

For the first time in her life, Della did not have a man telling her what to do and how to do it. She was no longer her father's household slave. She was no longer her alcoholic husband's abused wife. She could cook whenever and wherever and whatever she wanted to eat. She didn't have to sit in a chair and listen to her grandfather's non-stop preaching from Saturday sunset to Monday sunrise.

With her limited means she brightened the house using her talent and skill to create beautiful crocheted and tatted lace doilies and edging for pillowcases. A whiz at threading her loom with different color thread and yarn for specific projects, she then pushed the shuttle back and forth keeping her feet on the pedals making the screens swing back and forth. The designs and dreams that she stored in her imagination magically appeared as tablecloths, placemats on the kitchen table, and blankets hung over the living room couch for us to use on cold winter nights. She advertised her custom weaving in the Herald and News classified section and made custom placemats and table runners to match her customers' china.

In charge of her life at last, Della discovered she was intelligent and competent and she validated her new image by her actions. Although she wanted to work, her grade school education and the 1950s expectations for women severely limited her opportunities and earning capacity.

Della had the courage to apply for a nursing position at the Klamath County Infirmary. In 1951, at age fifty-six, she was hired. As a wife, it would have been unthinkable for her to work outside the home. That would have been an insult to her husband announcing to the world that he didn't make enough money to support his family. As a widow, however, those expectations changed and Della could work as a nurse's assistant without judgment from her peers. The social and legal status of women was slowly evolving.

This was after the Fair Labor Act established a minimum wage for women in 1938, but before Title VII of the Civil Rights Act was approved in 1964, prohibiting employment discrimination against women. However, according to the Women's History Project, a "nationwide discussion" about women's rights was raising the consciousness about gender discrimination in the 1950s.

The awakening national consciousness about women's legal rights certainly did not hinder her getting a job at age fifty-six. Della worked at the Klamath County Infirmary until she moved to Salem to be near her son, Dean, and his family. She then worked in a Salem hospital until age seventy-two.

I can't say with certainty that the employment discrimination protections passed in 1964 helped Della stay in the work force at a much older age than the average retiree. Della supported herself financially and made friends—trusting in happiness for the first time in her life. She gained the respect of her peers as a caring nursing professional. Della no longer thought of herself as a woman without value or rights.

It was amazing to see Della change her life, to blossom like a rose frozen in bud for a very long time. Our image of each other became more compatible and our relationship as mother and daughter improved during my last year in high school. She wasn't angry all the time and there wasn't a fight as soon as I opened the door about what I'd done wrong that day or year or lifetime. No more "If it wasn't for you…" As her self-esteem grew, she no longer used violence to communicate.

Despite limited business experience other than custom weaving, and selling eggs and the hams she cured and smoked, Della sold our country house and made sure the price was high enough to buy the house she wanted in town. She had to have had the second deal almost sealed before she finalized the first one. That took intelligence that had been hidden too long, some maneuvering, and the courage to take a risk hoping for a better future.

Della sought advice from her banker on how to handle the paperwork for both sales, just as she would later go to her banker for advice about stock investments after she moved to Salem. She was smart enough to know what she didn't know and ask for help. That's more than just pretty good for someone with an eighth-grade education and no work experience except childcare, housework, and farm labor. She also had the courage to try something new and different—she learned to swim at age seventy four with the help of two plastic bubbles that my husband, Chet, put together for her so she could float and not have to be afraid of going under water.

Since I had spent most of my life trying to avoid Della, I didn't really get to know her until after she suffered a stroke. Counseling had helped me trust enough to try getting closer to her, and her attitude had improved even more than after my father died. She visited me in the Portland area occasionally but it was difficult with her work schedule and having to travel from Salem by bus. With three, and then five grandsons for her to visit, we had very little time alone as mother and daughter.

In 1973, my husband, Chet, and I were on our annual ski vacation in Utah when we received a telephone call from a physician at Salem Memorial

Hospital. The doctor said that mother had suffered a cerebral vascular accident (CVA), or stroke. She was conscious and could talk, but had some paralysis of her hand and arm, and he had ordered that she be transferred to a nursing home within twenty-four hours. To him, she was just an old woman in a coveted hospital bed.

We arranged to have our Della transferred by ambulance from Salem Memorial Hospital to the Rehabilitation Institute of Oregon (RIO) in Portland. There the focus would be stroke recovery instead of warehousing her until she died. The Salem doctor did not order any laboratory tests until I told him we were transferring her to RIO. He didn't want Portland physicians to see that he had written off a patient as a worthless old *w*oman. With therapy she regained use of her hand and arm.

After a month, Della had stabilized and we moved her to an intermediate care facility called The Village. Her three-month stay went well until a nurse tried to coax her into joining other patients who were singing hymns. "Don't you want to be a sweet, little old lady?" she asked. Della's indignant reply was, "I can't think of anything I'd rather be less than a sweet little old lady!"

When Della was a patient at Willamette View Manor, the only assisted living facility then available in the Portland area, she started calling to tell me the nurses ignored her medical complaints. Since the symptoms seemed to go away when I visited her, I realized that Della was afraid we might abandon her. I promised her she could always count on two phone calls a day, my Wednesday visits, as well as her visits to our home every Sunday. She stopped complaining about nonexistent problems and for the first time in our lives we actually talked about the unfairness of her enslaved childhood and her life as a young woman, how that compared with being a wife and mother, and finally as an aging woman in failing health. As a woman who had been a caregiver for most of her seventy-nine years, she was now cared for and loved unconditionally. It was a long time coming and I think it made it easier for her to face her death.

On May 23, 1975, a Thursday evening, a year and a half after Della's stroke, I had a gut feeling I should go see her. Thursday evening was not our regular visiting schedule, but the feeling was urgent. When I arrived at the Manor, her room was empty. Della was downstairs in the nursing care section because she had a boil under her arm and needed more care than was available in the assisted-living area.

Della was absolutely furious about having to leave her room and her cherished quilts, her favorite rocking chair, and her aquarium for what she called, "the nursing home." She said, "I just think I'll have another stroke." Being a woman of her word, that's exactly what she did. She had a severe stroke and was dead by morning.

I am grateful my mother, Della Angia Augustus, had a second chance at life and I am grateful we had the opportunity to mend our relationship. She had finally defined her own life—not her father or grandfather or husband or nurses coaxing her to be a "sweet, little old lady." After a lifetime of enslavement and abuse, she knew she deserved happiness. My parents were victims of times in which they lived.

Della Angia Augustus and Lester A. Augustus went from enslavement to freedom in their lifetimes. While Della at her worst was abusive and at her best was stern, harsh, and uncaring, she was also responsible and reliable. My drunken father, Lester, at his worst gambled and lost the money that should have gone to care for his family, but at his best when he was sober, I could always count on him for love and encouragement, unlike my mother, Della. However, it was my mother's steadiness and perseverance that kept us afloat. Now I appreciate those values more than I resent her anger, her abuse, and her coldness toward me.

Della and Lester's childhoods were even worse than mine. I can't say with any honesty that I would have been less angry and less desperate if I had been abused sexually and not allowed to go to school. Our country has faced up to the evil of enslaving black men and women, but white women's enslavement in the United States of America has been a very well-kept secret.

I was embarrassed that I didn't know this sorry part of our history, but I have friends who are attorneys who had never heard of the 1971 Supreme Court ruling granting women legal status as persons, or the 1981 ruling that overturned several State laws that gave husbands unilateral control over jointly owned property, or the ruling in 1996 that finally clarified and left no doubts about women's legal rights. None of the three rulings were included in my friend's law school curriculum. The custom of enslaving the oldest daughter in the family is still a well-kept American secret.

I am proud to be the daughter of Lester A. Augustus and Della Angia Augustus.

Della Angia Augustus had one last secret. In 1999, her name was included in an "Oregon Division of State Lands - Unclaimed Property" newspaper advertisement. The unclaimed property was a Value Line Mutual Fund with my sister, Marjory, listed as the beneficiary. The bond company had no record of the mutual fund purchase in question so it was not legal for me to sell the shares. Only a nonprofit organization could legally redeem the mutual fund and only one nonprofit seemed appropriate: the Japanese Garden Society of Oregon.

All three Augustus women had appreciated the lovely Japanese Garden in Washington Park. I used to take Mother to their annual Mother's Day event and Marjory especially loved the iris garden with its offset geometric wooden planks leading you through the garden. It was her favorite place to visit when she was in Portland.

If you enter the garden on the path that leads up the hill from the entrance, you will see our names engraved on a wonderful stone located just inside the gate. I'm certain the three Augustus women all agree that it was money well spent.

1. Left Della Augustus 2. DeVoss Family Home 3. Windy Ridge School 4. Waterville, Kansas
5. Waterville Methodist Church 6. Walter, Lloyd, Father Edward, George, Leonard DeVoss
7. Carolyn and Della DeVoss 8. Elmer Augustus 9. Della and Lester Augustus 10. Lester Augustus
11. Marjory and Dean Augustus in Kansas

46

1. Della Augustus. 2. Front left: Murray Dean Augustus, Grandfather Edward DeVoss. Back left:
Della Augustus, Dean Augustus. 3. Anna and Della Augustus. 4. Center: Frank Augustus. 5. Frank
and Ida Augustus. 6. Augustus brothers, Front left: Herbert, Guy, Harold. Back left: Elmer, Lester.
7. Lester and Mother Ida. 8. McMillan Mansion. 9. Lester's sod roof home after he ran away

1. No widow's peaks: My sister Marge, uncle Lloyd DeVoss, aunt Doris Whitney
2. Gussie's widow's peak, just like her father's.

1. Lester and his racehorses. 2. Lester in Parker, Colorado. 3. Lester and his winning greyhounds.
4. Lester and friends with racing greyhound. 5. Lester's daughter, Dorothy and wife, Iva. 6. Iva
Augustus. 7. Dorothy, Iva, Lester fishing. 8. Basin Mining Company in Rocky Mountains.
9. Norma (Gussie) and brother, Dean in Montana. 10. Lester and Norma (Gussie) fishing in
Missouri River. 11. Madison River Dam.

1. Gussie's catch of the day. 2. Lester, Gussie, Della at Fairhaven, Oregon. 3. Lester duck hunting. 4. Gussie and Lester at house by golf course in Klamath Falls, Oregon. 5. Lester and Lady-Black Laborador. 6. Pudge, Chesapeake. 7. Lester in his beloved garden. 8. Ethel, Lester's sister. 9. DeVoss family reunion: Front left: Della, Lloyd, Carolyn, George, Doris, Walter. 10. Dorothy, Della, Norma and Augustus after Lester's funeral. 11. Dorothy, Della, Norma at Lester's gravesite in Klamath Falls, Oregon.

1. Della Augustus at work Klamath County Infirmary. 2. Della after stroke in McRobert Japanese entry garden. 3. Stone commemorating lost property mutual fund $21,000 donation to Japanese Garden in Portland, Oregon. 4. Japanese Garden Pavilion.

Chapter Three
The Unwanted Daughter

I have only one memory of my life in Colorado: the cave where the chopped river ice was stored during the summer. I have pieced together parts of my life from talking with Marge and from photographs of a little girl playing in the water, feeding the chickens, playing with her cousins, Bill and Duane, and proudly showing off a new dress. However, there was an undercurrent that can't be found in any of the Colorado photos: Mother broke the unwritten rules of her family, her church, and the Kansas community in which she lived when she gave birth to a daughter too long after her husband was killed by a lightning strike.

It wasn't socially acceptable for an unmarried woman to give birth to a baby in Kansas or any other state. Both the mother and the baby were stigmatized and labeled as improper, not meeting the standards and expectations of the proper communities in which they lived.

The response was either rejection as championed by Reverend Isaac DeVoss, or silence and secrets, which was the choice of Della and Lester Augustus. In the 21st century, studies by the Institute of American Values show most unwed mothers are pregnant by choice and are accepted by friends and family. My parents were stigmatized and went into hiding by moving to Montana.

With the same last name, Augustus, it was easy for my mother and father to pass as a married couple. However, common law marriage was, and is today, legal in Colorado and Montana. Even though Oregon never permitted such marriages, Lester and Della's relationship would have been recognized as legal in Oregon because it began in another state that allowed common law marriage. Their relationship would have been legal in any state under "conflict and choice-of-law statutes."

In Blanca, however, there was another problem. My birth more than nine months after her husband's death couldn't be hidden from the farming community even with a home delivery. Nice women simply did not get themselves in positions that led to pregnancy and giving birth to illegitimate children.

In Montana, they could start a new life where nobody knew anything about them or the birth status of their daughter; however, four family secrets traveled with them. One family secret is a burden. Four are absolute misery. My family had four secrets: 1) My father's birth father was not his mother's husband; 2) My controversial and untimely birth; 3) Mother's murder attempts; and 4) My parents lack of a marriage license.

Hiding family secrets creates dysfunctional families. Exposing family secrets takes away their power to distort relationships. Our family's dysfunctional structure depended upon my mother accepting the role of queen in charge of hiding our secrets. Our Queen Mother used the usual dysfunctional trio of tools to control us and keep us in line—shame, blame, and anger. Fear is the typical response of the person labeled as the family secret. In our case, that was the youngest daughter.

My mother's anger was a very real part of my daily life. Whether it was flogging me with a bunch of carrots freshly picked from the garden, a stick of wood recently chopped, the broom, or anything else that was handy, Mother made it clear I was not her favorite person. Everything bad that happened to her in the course of a day became my fault—"If it wasn't for you...."

If she broke a dish or blew up the pressure cooker or the chickens got out or a neighbors cattle broke through our fence, she would scream at me as though I was the cause of the problem. I was the safety valve that kept her reservoir of rage from overflowing onto others.

I feared for my life from the time I awoke in the morning until I went to sleep at night. It was like being in hell without the flames. My response was to spend as little time with her as possible—I escaped to hideaways in the Rocky Mountains of Montana and then the green fields of Oregon. It was a case of trying to escape physically from a psychological nightmare. I was a sleepwalker, which sleep experts say can be caused by emotional stress and anxiety. My sleepwalking nights ended sometime during my freshman year in high school as I settled into the supportive atmosphere of Henley High School.

Mother wanted me to succeed, but not too much. She was pleased to see mostly A's on my report card, yet an occasional B was even better. Her experience was that too much success or happiness would trigger a negative reaction, and she passed this expectation onto me. So I was hurt but not surprised that Mother never recognized in any way that her daughter Norma Jean Augustus was valedictorian of her high school graduating class. Silence was better than beatings.

Too much success also started the father-warden indoctrination tape that still played in her head—the one that insisted that women were second-class beings and warned her to not let me grow up to be an uppity woman who thought she was equal to men.

Mother was inconsistent. Did she feel guilty for her abuse when she made her fabulous raised donuts for me and timed them so they were fresh and warm when I got home from school? That was one of the good times. But bad times always followed good times as the cycle began again. That routine created a dysfunctional demon in my psyche and later in life I would feel uneasy during happy times unconsciously expecting the "crash" I had been taught would follow. I had to pay a price for enjoying the good times.

I preferred avoidance to confrontation, and Mother's silence to her "on again-off-again" interest in me. I had not yet delved into my battered psyche when I first learned about my untimely birth. I was thirty-one, recently divorced from an abusive and violent man and I was hanging onto my very life by my fingernails. I couldn't relive my terror-filled childhood without reliving my disastrous and terror-filled marriage. Terror is terror no matter what the source, and I wanted to forget my sentence of hell with my first husband, Marshall Francis Brown, M.D.

I didn't have the psychological tools to frame the question, much less talk to my mother about this new information. I was the perfect scapegoat. My silence protected our family secret, which I would learn later was simply unfinished psychological business. I buried what my sister in-law, Johnnie, told me about my birth status deep in my memory bank where it would fester for another ten years before I discussed it with my sister, Marjory.

Finally, after several years of working with a good counselor, I had healed enough that I was finally able to ask Marjory if the story my sister-in-law had told me about my birth status was true. She confirmed Johnnie's portrayal of Mother's pregnancy after her husband, Elmer, was killed and then said, "But we loved you."

"But we loved you" wasn't an answer to my question and it didn't make sense so I asked the million dollar follow-up question: "What do you mean?"

Then Marjory ended the cover-up and silence that had kept Mother's secret—very secret—for forty-one years. She told me everything, straightforward with no hedging or excuses about Mother's soap opera murder attempts. I didn't tell her about the floggings and beatings.

I should have confronted Mother because I knew that dealing with "unfinished psychological business" was vital for sound mental health. Until you confront the issue and talk it through, it stays unresolved. I wasn't up to resolving it at that point in time.

How do you ask your mother if she tried to kill you? Would you really want to know the answer to that question? What would you say if the answer was yes? I wasn't up to hearing the truth about that part of our lives. She died a year later, ending the possibility of ever hearing her side of the story. I had to work through it by myself.

I knew from early childhood that my mother hated me with a passion. She let me know that every day. But I didn't know why. She couldn't display anger or displeasure about her nineteen-year sentence as the household slave, and she was not going to quietly accept being enslaved another twenty years with an unwanted child. Every day began and ended with her angry accusations: "If it wasn't for you...." My response was escape and avoidance. That kept me safe but gave me no experience with other problem solving methods. As an adult, I had to learn how to mediate and resolve disagreements through counseling and trial and error.

I have attempted to preserve the good memories of my childhood, but I was denied some mementoes that would have helped me remember the good times. When my father died, Mother gave one of his prize possessions, not to his daughter, but to his nephew, Dean. The prized possession was a hundred-year-old medical book. My father used to read his favorite remedies aloud to us. The one I remember is the recommended cure for appendicitis: a spoonful of cayenne pepper followed by sleeping in the stable with the cows and horses, which was always followed by much laughter by everyone in the room.

Dean thought so little of my father's prized book that he later sold it without even offering it to me. Was the book a reminder of the man whom he probably blamed for his mother's fall from grace? If he had given or sold the book to me, would the reminder of the owner continue to eat at his heart and his soul? Or did Dean sell the book as a payback for my father and his mother's sexual fervor, which came much too soon after his father's death? It could have been to make a few dollars, I don't know. I didn't have the insight or the courage to ask Dean those questions before he died.

I was surprised and dismayed when I learned Mother had given my prized clarinet to my cousin after I left for nursing school without asking me or even telling me about her misplaced generosity. I dragged a tuba through the snow all winter and practiced every day to show I deserved that clarinet. It was special and we had an eight-year history—we knew each other well. I had a special feel for the keys knowing just how much lung pressure and finger play it took for each note to sound its best. It was like an old friend had been taken away from me. Many years later, my second and forever husband, Chet, gave me a clarinet for my birthday, but it wasn't the same. You just can't replace an old friend.

Now, I see Mother's uncaring actions as symbolic of our entire relationship. I was not a son—I was only a worthless daughter, a non-entity and a non-person without value or rights. I was the mirror image of her— a painful reminder of the inequities and injustice she endured as the oldest daughter in the DeVoss family for so many years.

Disposing of my personal property could have been symbolic of her attempts to dispose of me as an infant. Clearly, she had no respect for my personal boundaries. She played the same life game and tapes she inherited from her parents and grandparents.

When I was three, we moved to Montana where nobody knew about her unplanned pregnancy. The Lester A. Augustus family arrived in Basin in the dead of winter. The snow was so high that the only way to get out outside was through a tunnel shoveled by my father. It wasn't easy to get around on foot for a three-year-old and her mother. So we stayed inside and Mother ate until spring arrived, and when she emerged from her hibernation she had gained thirty pounds. Mother kept the girdle she wore when she arrived for years as proof that she was once slim and trim.

I know we had at least one magazine and a newspaper in our snowbound house, because she read the same thing to me over and over for hours at a time. By spring I could read along with her. She was proud she had taught me to read when I was only four years old. The burden of being the fallen woman seemed to be lifted by a new life away from anyone who knew about her past—and the beauty of the Rocky Mountains was a bonus.

Nothing can compare with the sights that awaited us in our first Montana springtime. Imagine the snow-covered mountains that surrounded and protected the mining camp just exploding with purple crocuses. The other children and I picked as many as we could carry and took them home to our mothers. In summer, a new magic act astounded us with mountainsides covered with wild orchids. We carried them home to our mothers, too. I thought it was heaven.

Playmates, mostly boys, were plentiful in our neighborhoods and I was home only for meals and at bedtime. In the summer we hiked out of the basin up higher into the Rocky Mountains and lay in the grass looking up at the blue sky and the clouds. We explored the dilapidated empty buildings we called our ghost town. We made whistles from willow trees, played dress-up, and sang "Hand Me Down My Walking Cane" on the stage of an abandoned saloon. I don't remember who had the costumes, but the girls wore fancy long dresses and a boy did, in fact, have a "walking cane" that he swung as he strutted and the girls danced across the stage. I used to think if I could come back for another turn on this Earth, I'd like to be a dancing girl in New York.

As we were having fun running and playing in the year-round sunshine in the Rocky Mountains, our fathers labored in the dark. The mine was deep, deep in the ground. An elevator took the miners down to whatever section was being mined that day. They had small lamps strapped on their hard hats. They carried a black metal candleholder about seven or eight inches long and sharpened on the end so it could be forced into the mine wall. I used one as a candleholder much later before giving it, along with other mining memorabilia, to my sons as keepsakes to remember my father.

We children didn't go near that mine. We were warned against it and that was one time we all did as we were told. But there was another mineshaft down the road from the Basin camp that was horizontal and I have to admit that we did venture inside that one. Not too far. It was scary! I've wondered if it is the Merry Widow mine in Basin where people pay to breathe the radon gas hoping to cure their arthritis. The AllPosters.com website shows people sitting on either side of the mine and it looks pretty much as I remember it as our adventure of the week.

In the winter we rode our sleds down the hill to the creek. I always stayed outside too long in the subzero Montana temperatures. Mother would pour warm water over my hands and feet when I returned home to prevent frostbite damage, but even now my extremities overreact to being exposed to cold temperatures— turning white and painful enough to remind me of my Montana winters.

I remember once when I couldn't resist a dare and I had to walk up the hill with my tongue frozen to the metal part of my sled. More warm water helped my tongue, but not my state of embarrassment.

Alcohol and gambling addictions controlled my father. There was no medical understanding of alcoholism as a disease. There were no treatment programs available or Twelve Step programs for either the alcoholic or family members. So Della tried to figure out how to live with Lester day by day. She ended up playing into his illness by trying to cure it with "if I did *this* differently or if I did *that* more often maybe he wouldn't drink." She didn't know that she didn't cause his alcoholism, she couldn't control it, and she couldn't cure it. It would be years before she was released from the torment of alcoholism.

As my father's drinking grew out of control, mother's angry accusations of "If it wasn't for you…" began as an Augustus family ritual. Not even frosty winter weather with thermometers registering forty degrees below zero kept me inside. Why would my mother let me, at age four or five, play outside in temperatures cold enough to freeze me to death? Was it a continuation of her "kitchen counter" tricks in Blanca? I really don't want to know the answers to those questions.

My male playmates didn't treat me differently because I was a girl. I was just part of the gang of kids. I do remember two boys who were my age trying to take off my clothes to see what girls looked like when I was four or five. I didn't understand what was going on exactly but I knew I didn't like it and I wanted it to stop. I distracted them with a promise that my mother's famous peanut butter fudge awaited us at my house. Up the hill we went!

That episode created a warning mechanism in my brain—the feeling that something utterly wrong is about to happen and I'd better do something to avoid the consequences. I call this my "Montana Distrust Signal." It was to become a factor in my relationships with men.

I completed the first and second grade at Boulder Elementary School. School was a place where I felt safe. There was no screaming or hitting. I remember taking a meal in a jar so the teacher could warm it for lunch in a big kettle, playing the tambourine in the school band, and getting caught in a lie sitting in the front row in the first grade. I don't remember what it was I lied about. I do remember being absolutely mortified. That experience kept me from straying too far from the truth from that day to this day.

We moved to Southern Oregon when I was seven years old to be near Dean and Marjory. Their emotional support gave me a sense of security and visits to them gave me my first experience of living in a non-alcoholic environment. But our mother must have been concerned by their presence because they knew about our family secrets. Would they tell me about her murder attempts? How would she handle my question if I asked her about the kitchen counter escapades?

Life in Oregon revolved around the very basic elements of daily life. We first lived in a small town called Keno. It is mostly a blur to me except that school lunch was cafeteria food. No more bringing a lunch-in-a-jar from home. There were tantalizing frosting covered maple bars. I had never even seen such things, much less tasted them. I would have eaten a dozen at one sitting if the cafeteria cooks had looked the other way.

Then we moved to a neighborhood near the Fairhaven Elementary School. Here I was welcomed by another group of kids, mostly boys, and again we roamed all day unsupervised. In the summer, I wore bib overalls and went barefoot. I always played first base in our ball games because the base was a tree and I could be in the shade. I still have scarred knees from bicycle falls onto gravel roads. I remember pulling a thumbtack out of my heel one night in the shower. My calluses were so thick I didn't even know it was there. All my friends were boys—I was just one of the gang.

I loved school because both the teachers and the students welcomed the girl from Montana. It was at Fairhaven, however, where I had my first lesson about discrimination—being different wasn't acceptable.

In gym class there was a girl who was not welcome. She was an ordinary girl like the rest of us except for her hands. Her fingers had rounded extensions with no fingernails. They looked like little, round, skin-covered balls. They didn't hinder her in any way. She could write and catch balls but nobody wanted to hold hands with her when we were forming a circle to play a game. I was absolutely stunned by my fellow and sister student's actions. I left my place in the circle, walked toward her, held out my hand, and reached for hers. I still remember the look in her eyes. It was a look of disbelief and gratitude. I would give anything to remember her name and I hope her adult life was better than her childhood.

It wasn't the last incident of discrimination I saw at Fairhaven. Class attendance year to year was pretty consistent but one girl only attended school in the fall and spring. Her parents were Caucasian migrant workers who followed the crops. Her name was Norma Dean and she is the only Norma I've ever known with a middle name other than Jean. I was impressed. My fellow students didn't treat her as badly as the other girl but they let it be known that they wondered about her coming and going. Again, I didn't see why it mattered.

Now I wonder if I knew instinctively that I was different as well. I had not yet been told the story of my beginnings, but something inside me rebelled against treating people badly just because they were different from the norm. It is a belief that guides my life to this day.

That belief became even stronger when I saw with my own eyes the horror of the Tulelake, California Japanese "internment" camp located just south of the Klamath County borderline. Internment was the term used by our federal government to describe the camp. My parents took me with them to see what local residents called "the concentration camp."

It was a sunny day. People were walking outside within the confines of a barbed wire fence. They lived in barracks covered with black tarpaper. There wasn't a tree in sight to provide shade and summer temperatures sometimes reached 106 degrees. Tulelake water was tainted with sulfur strong enough to stink to high heaven and stain anything it touched. It made me nauseated to even think of having to drink it. But what scared me the most were the soldiers standing in towers high above the prisoners with guns ready to shoot anyone who tried to escape. It was a frightening experience for a ten-year-old girl.

You may be thinking, "Could she really remember this or is she making it up?" Horror-filled events brand such sights and conversations in our memory banks. While the concentration camp isn't something I think about every day, I do think of it when I see something happening that is unfair, and it provokes a replay of what I saw that horrible day.

School didn't save the Japanese children from concentration camps, but school and good teachers saved me from sinking into the chaos of my dysfunctional family. Teachers made no distinction between boys and girls. Expectations were clear. Intelligence was valued and never ridiculed. My family secret didn't matter. School broadened my understanding of the world around me and gave me hope for the future.

Maude Melton, my fifth-grade teacher, was an especially amazing woman. She almost died from scarlet fever as a child and had to wear a wig to cover her baldness. She also had a wooden leg, but she never let her stiff gait or difficulty in bending handicap her in any way. She would laugh about it if it didn't work properly, "There it goes again!"

She taught me, and I hope the students who wouldn't touch the disfigured hands of the girl in gym class, that it was okay to be different and that such difficulties could be overcome. She taught us to be true to our values. The first thing we did every morning before class started was stand next to our desks, raise our right hand, and recite her version of a Shakespeare' quote: "To thine own self be true, for as day follows night, you cannot be false to anyone." A copy of her pledge hangs on my office wall to remind me daily of her good advice. Maude Melton taught me well.

Music and playing in the band further expanded my narrow world and added to my experience of boys and girls treated as equals. I wanted very much to play clarinet in the Fairhaven Elementary School band. My father promised me he would buy me a clarinet if I played a school instrument for a period of time to prove to him I was serious. The only school instrument available at the time was a tuba. We had to walk to and from school. I carried and dragged a tuba case that was almost as tall as I was home every night. Then I carried and dragged it back to school the next day, even through snow. I practiced the tuba faithfully every night for six months and my father bought me a clarinet. That was an important moment in my life. My father had made a promise and he kept it. It was a time I could depend on him.

The band teacher at Altamont Junior High School had one test to select the first-chair clarinet. It was the tone of one note held for a period of time. He selected me to be first-chair clarinet and I was terrified I wasn't up to the honor. My father paid for weekly lessons that helped me meet the maestro's expectations. The underlying message was that quality performance was more important than gender.

My Henley High School experience would reinforce what I had learned at Boulder and Fairhaven Elementary Schools, and Altamont Junior High School. Gender didn't matter and violence was unacceptable. I didn't tell anyone at school about mother's angry rages or her beatings. I suspect Mother worried that I might talk about what went on in our house of horrors when we were alone, and that fear might have accounted for our few "good times."

The Henley High School teachers and Board of Directors believed in gender equality. The only class girls could not take was Physics and that was because the beleaguered coach who also taught Physical Education and Chemistry wanted to limit the class size. Boys could take Home Economics. Girls could take Shop. Girls played competitive sports. I doubt that school officials considered the women's rights movement when they established their policies to guide how the school would be run. It was simply a common-sense way to operate a small country school district.

Everything about Henley counteracted the alcoholic dysfunction I had learned from my parents. Students were all expected to be capable and reliable. We learned to think strategically and take action when necessary. These assets helped me as a wife and mother and were also vital in helping me succeed in various careers as a nurse, broadcast journalist, and mayor.

Henley teachers also taught personal responsibility. The Student Council had the last word on punishment for student misbehavior. They were tough—my sentence for skipping school as a junior to go with a friend on senior skip day was two weeks of detention after school. There was no after school transportation so I had to walk home from school because Mother refused to come and get me.

Students took Office Practice as a class and earned credits for answering phones and managing the office paperwork. There were no paid secretaries. The student body elected a treasurer choosing between candidates who had taken bookkeeping classes for at least two years. The treasurer did the daily bookkeeping, and wrote the checks to pay the bills, but didn't sign them. That was the principal's responsibility. A Certified Public Accountant came once a week to oversee the students' work. I had the honor of being elected school treasurer during my senior year.

Teachers talked about the ups and downs we could expect in life. The message was to be honest and straightforward, work toward success, and not to worry about defeat or failure since they are only temporary conditions. I applied those principles to my life at home and they gave me hope. They work for me today as well as they did then.

That concept was also important in playing competitive sports against two other small southern Oregon high schools and being part of a team. We were taught to respect competitors on and off the field. I learned that women could be competitive in a positive way, from playing left end on the football team, high jumping on the track team, or boring girls'-rules basketball (no dribbling the ball down the court).

I learned the hard way that when I got knocked down, I could get up and go on. I had already learned that lesson from my mother, but somehow these new experiences made the hidden part of my life easier.

We were taught to respect competitors on and off the field. Creating opposing arguments on the debate team made us appreciate different opinions. We learned to research our assigned issue, organize the information, not get distracted by badgering questions, and sell our product. These Henley lessons have served me well in everyday life, as the mother of five sons, and particularly during my time as mayor.

Dating customs were much different then they are today. Henley High School had 250 students including seventh and eighth graders. Nobody went "steady" and nobody organized our pairings on a spreadsheet. It just ended up that on Monday you went out with A, Tuesday it was B, and so on through the seven-day week. It seemed to me that it was boys and girls as just friends—no romance. Or it may have been my Montana Distrust Signal at work. A classmate, Charlie "Bud" Shulmire, clarified my behavior at a high school reunion years later. He told my husband, Chet McRobert, that my reputation was above reproach. Since Charlie and I never dated, my reservation must have been a topic of conversation when the guys hung out. I tried sex once to see what all the fuss was about. I was under-whelmed. Chet McRobert would later teach me all I needed to know about that subject.

My fascination with dancing began when I played dress-up in Montana and it continued in Oregon, big time. It was the Big Band era and the bands flew regularly up and down the West Coast. Luckily for us, airplanes at the time couldn't go from San Francisco to Portland without refueling at Kingsley Field Airport in Klamath Falls. The big bands played a gig on Saturday nights in the armory. We danced to the Dorsey brothers, Woody Herman, Lionel Hampton, and many others. If it was Saturday night in Klamath Falls it was time to jitterbug. On my birthday one year, we danced to the Ralph Flanagan Band. Years later, when I was on better terms with my mother, I remember thinking she had probably gone without something to have enough money to buy me the particular brown dress I wore to that birthday dance.

Henley High School's small student body was definitely an advantage. Ours was the last small class before three rural school districts merged into one larger district for cost efficiency. I often wonder if this affected the Henley way of getting along with people. With only twenty-three students in our class, there weren't enough of us to form cliques. Everyone was your friend even if there was something improper about your family.

Careers for women were limited when I graduated from high school. My Henley High School Senior Handbook listed employment options by gender. Women could become actresses and dancers, bookkeepers, accountants, cashiers, nurses, ticket agents, sales women, semiskilled factory workers, servants, stenographers, typists, secretaries, teachers, and waitresses.

No women architects. No women aviators. No women dentists. No women engineers. No women lawyers or judges. No women truck drivers or chauffeurs. No women physicians. No women surgeons. These professions were listed as options for boys only.

It was a surprise to see limitations for girls in a Henley document. It seemed out of step with the boys and girls are equal treatment I had experienced but it was a refection of the reality of the workplace.

At the end of my senior year in high school I applied for a four-year college scholarship sponsored by the Klamath County Elks Lodge. It was a countywide competition open to both girls and boys. The requirements were clear. There were specific things you had to have accomplished. My teachers were quite sure that I met the requirements and would receive the scholarship. I did receive a letter from the Elks Scholarship Committee congratulating me for making the highest score of anyone, but because they thought a boy would contribute more to society than I could as a girl, they had awarded the scholarship to the applicant with the second highest score, a male.

That message was crystal clear. It was acceptable for girls to succeed within certain parameters, but if they stepped outside those boundaries, they should expect harsh consequences. That was my first inkling that there might be challenges ahead.

I had no idea then how valuable my Henley country girl life skills would be as I faced life in the city.

1. Norma watering the chickens in Waterville, Kansas. 2. Norma, not crying. 3. Norma loves her beautiful pink silk dress. 4. Norma riding a saddle wishing it was a horse. 5. Norma in Colorado Springs on the way to Montana. 6. Montana Basin mine in winter. 7. Norma and unknown girl enjoying snow in June. 8. Norma in area where miners lived. 9. Lester teasing Norma.

1. In costumes for musical play in abandoned theatre: Unknown girl, Norma, unknown girl.
2. Norma's catch of the day on the Missouri River. 3. Norma playing tambourine at Boulder, Montana elementary school. 4. Left: Cousin Carolyn DeVoss, Norma, Dora Jean DeVoss in Keno, Oregon. 5. Norma with Marge's bicycle. 6. Norma in Fairhaven neighborhood. 7. Norma and Murray Dean at her brother's house. 8. Norma and Lester's house by golf course with Kesterson Lumber Mill smoke stack. 9. Norma and Della house on highway to California. 10. Norma dressed up in I. Magnin suit in Berkeley, California. 11. Henley High School.

1. George Elliott, Henley High School Principal. 2 Henley Student Council, Gussie third from left.
3. Henley Girls Team Points, Gussie first row far right. 4. Henley Girls Athletic Association, Gussie
front row far left. 5. Henley Pep Club, Gussie Top row, fifth from right. 6. Henley Glee Cub,
Gussie fourth row second from right. 7. Henley Band, Gussie top row third from right.

1. Henley Spring Play - Bicycle Built for Two, Gussie second from right.
2. Full cast of Spring Play, Gussie top row, sixth from right.
3. Norma (Gussie) McRobert, Valedictorian.
4. Year patch to go with letterwoman's sweater.

CHAPTER FOUR

THE FAVORED SON

D ean's favored son position came with a hidden underbelly of secrets and promises. Dean walked a fine line. He prevented his Mother from killing me, but he protected her by keeping our third family secret, her attempted murder of her infant daughter, very secret. He was in a no win situation created by his mother. He was damned if he spoke up, and he was damned if he kept quiet.

At age eighteen, Dean lost his father, Elmer, and with little time to grieve his death had been confronted with his mother's pregnancy. Unlike mother, Dean did not blame me for being born or for any feelings of betrayal he might have had. I had three wonderful years of his doting love and affection when he stayed home from school to protect me from our mother. Later, after we moved from Montana to Oregon to be near my brother and sister, Mother never raged at me or beat me when they were around. I adored my big brother and my sister.

Dean had additional responsibilities at home after his father was killed. In addition to going to school, he fed the livestock, milked the cows, and cleaned and shoveled out the barn. Wood had to be cut for heating and cooking. Water from a central pump had to be carried to the house—a chore he shared with his mother. In the spring, he went with the neighborhood men to chop river ice with an axe. All the river ice was stored in a nearby underground cave. Dean carried ice chunks to the house every day to replenish the icebox and keep food from spoiling—especially Mother's homemade cottage cheese that I was told I ate by the handfuls with glee. My only memory of Colorado is going to the cave to get ice for Mother to make homemade ice cream.

Dean graduated from high school in Blanca, Colorado. After his sister, Marge graduated from Business School, they moved to Klamath Falls, Oregon. He found work as an accountant, and met his future wife, Juanita Dahms also known as Johnnie. I was nine years old, and since Johnnie was just nine years older than me, I thought of her as an older sister. She added cheer to our sometimes less than cheerful household.

Dean and Johnnie were married in Reno, Nevada. Johnnie was eighteen years old. Dean was twenty-seven. Their honeymoon had to be put on hold because Dean wanted to serve his country. He didn't wait to be drafted. He joined the Seabees and was headed for the South Pacific. Dean was a Boatswain's Mate Second Class, V-6 and served in the 3rd, 10th, 16th, and 99th Naval Construction Battalions. We did get to see him in uniform—he looked so handsome. He came home on leave at least once that I remember, and he also met Johnnie in San Francisco where they celebrated with Marge and her fiancé, O. C. Davies. Dean was awarded an Asiatic-Pacific Ribbon and a Good Conduct Medal. We were relieved when the war ended and he returned home safe and sound. He was my protector. When he was home and a frequent visitor I felt safe and sound because Mother saved her violence to take out on me until later.

Dean and Johnnie had two sons, Murray Dean and Dennis Edward. At age twenty-two, Johnnie was pregnant with their third child when a friend who owned a log truck asked Dean to drive it for him for just one day. Dean took a day off from his accounting work to do his friend a favor—a favor that nearly cost him his life.

Those were the days when one, two, or three logs were big enough to make a load. That fateful day, Dean had a three-log load. When he tried to secure the load, the chain caught on a snag and pulled the top log off the truck onto him.

He survived, but his spinal cord was crushed and he was completely paralyzed from his waist to his feet. A local doctor, a general practitioner with no training in neurosurgery, ignored the pleas of our family to send Dean to Eugene where specialists were available. He performed surgery without the consent of my brother or his wife. He later lost his license to practice medicine,

A registered nurse cared for Dean in the daytime when he was discharged from the hospital. However, having to provide nursing care after the nurse left for the day, taking care of their two young sons, and being pregnant was a lot of responsibility for a twenty-two year old woman. She needed someone to help to give her some time for herself and to shop and do the things wives and mothers do.

I was fourteen at the time and devastated about the accident. With no discussion or concern about my feelings of loss, Mother informed me that I would be helping my brother's family every Saturday and Sunday.

I was expected to clean house, cook, and help with their sons. I did whatever needed to be done. My mother transferred payment of my family secret obligations to her son. She loaned me out to work as a servant just as her father had done with her. She probably thought it was light duty. Only two days a week of servitude for four years, compared to her sentence.

I didn't question her decision because I enjoyed my nephews. I looked forward to being with them and I wanted to help. Over time though, I wondered why my sister-in-law's younger sister, Iva Lee, didn't take a turn on Saturdays or Sundays or be there at 5:00 AM to help pick pin feathers and get the turkey ready for Thanksgiving and Christmas dinners.

It didn't seem fair. She was near my age, so that wasn't an issue. She wasn't handicapped, so that was no explanation. I decided she was just an innocent bystander. However, the family my brother had married into was just as wrapped up in dysfunctional maneuvers as ours was, which isn't surprising. He was simply going along with his mother and continuing the pattern she taught him. Now I believe it was part of my family secret scapegoat payback and Iva Lee was part of the package.

A friend and I took her to a basketball game in Klamath Falls because she didn't have transportation. We didn't sit together, but we agreed to meet after the game at a specific place to take her home. My friend and I waited and waited and waited for Iva Lee. Finally, we left without her.

Iva Lee told Johnnie that she had to walk home and that we didn't keep our promise. That meant I was in big trouble. I was grounded for weeks except on Saturday and Sunday when I did my usual chores: clean the house, do the laundry, iron the clothes, whatever needed to be done routine. I stayed as far away from Iva Lee as possible.

Formerly the family breadwinner, Dean was unable to work except for a short period of time during his twenty-four years as a paraplegic. While he still played a role in his children's lives he was not the same father they had known before the accident. Their family system was out of balance. In those days paraplegic families received no psychological or sexual counseling as they do today. They had to struggle through the problems caused by paralysis day by day without help from the medical community. They had to struggle through the problems caused by paralysis day by day without help from the medical community.

Johnnie loved Dean and showed real concern for him. But over time, the responsibility and changes in their emotional and physical relationship took a toll on her sense of well-being. Her youth when the accident happened made her adjustment even more difficult. She must have felt trapped. If she left Dean she would be severely criticized by friends and family. If she stayed with him she was a heroine but limited to a life that revolved around an invalid husband.

Johnnie often complained to me about her life. I assured her I would be responsible for his care if she wanted out of the relationship. She always rejected that option but didn't stop complaining. Dean acknowledged that Johnnie took his pain pills and mixed them with alcohol. He admitted her neglect was responsible for his weight loss, which forced his hospitalization every couple of months. But he defended her actions. He knew Johnnie was between a rock and a hard place—and he loved her.

Johnnie was in a no-win situation. So she exercised the only power she had—knowledge. Since Dean had told her about our dirty little family secrets, she must have thought we couldn't refuse her demands. The hidden threat that she might spill the beans about the Lester and Della Augustus family assured that the secret would remain secret. That was a classic family secret maneuver and it's called blackmailing the scapegoats. Blackmail may seem to be a little harsh but the actions are similar. If somebody knows something about you that they think you are ashamed of, they then expect you to do whatever they request to keep them quiet. It was a life-long game.

Johnnie complained constantly that their financial situation was grim, but we knew they received a substantial monthly payment from the Puckett Timber Company, and that Dean's medical expenses, which were costly, were covered by company insurance.

Yet my mother, sister, and I sent monthly checks. When Mother died, I found a letter to the "family," i.e., Dean and Johnnie. They had purchased a new car and expected her to pay for it as well as their house. She basically said the con was over. She wrote, "I love you but I am 72 years old and I am tired in more ways than one." The favored son era was over. Only two of the three Augustus women had fallen for the scam.

In 1964, Johnnie came to my home to tell me that Dean was concerned about me because I had divorced my husband of ten years. He thought I should know that I was born after my mother's first husband died and that Mother was not married to Lester at the time of my birth.

But if he told Johnnie about Mother's attempts to kill me, she kept it secret. Years later, when my sister, Marjory, told me about that chapter in my soap opera life I realized there were at least two reasons that Dean had chosen not to tell me the whole story at that time: 1. He thought my birth status was enough for my psyche to handle so soon after a messy divorce, and 2. He wanted to protect his mother's reputation.

If the first issue, my birth status, was his primary concern, he would have come forward later knowing I had healed from my abusive first marriage. Now I think his favored son training and role with all of its inherent denial of the facts about his mother was stronger than his concern for the truth. Again, he was in a no-win situation.

Dean played the favored son to the end, protected his mother's reputation and joined his wife as a player in the family secret scapegoat game. It was a difficult game to quit. I had been trained from birth to be the family scapegoat and to accept the blame for anything and everything my mother didn't like. I was the Augustus family patsy whether it was being the only younger sister to help on weekends, or as an adult, when the payoff was financial because the monthly checks continued with the occasional extra for whatever was their crisis of the day.

Chronic kidney infections plagued Dean and he had to quit his beloved accounting job. The antibiotics available were ineffective and he died twenty-four years after the accident at age fifty-six. I put on my nurses uniform and took care of him in his last siege— fighting for his life in a hospital bed. It was a special time for us and we were at peace with each other.

Life isn't always fair. But you move on. That was the lesson I learned from my big brother. I still think about him and I miss him. I planted a beautiful hydrangea plant that blossoms every spring in his honor.

I divorced my sister-in-law after my brother died. I checked out her last "the sky is falling" emergency phone call claiming that she was bleeding internally and needed several hundred dollars immediately. I explained the situation to her doctor and learned it was a blatant lie—she was not bleeding. I said "enough." I simply couldn't continue having to deal with her drama of the day and I vowed there would be no more money from me. That was the end of my role as the Augustus Family Secret Scapegoat.

Of course, Johnnie thought I was just being a troublemaker. She sent a grandson to ask me to welcome her back into my family. If she had ever expressed any remorse for her untruthfulness and neglect and mistreatment of my brother and shown a willingness to change, I would have felt differently. One nephew hasn't spoken to me since I ended the family secret game.

You could say Johnnie was a heroic figure. Barely out of her teen-age years when Dean's accident changed their life forever, she coped as best she could with the limited knowledge and services then available.

But I couldn't make up for the years she had lost. And I couldn't give her the support she would have had if Dean had been injured years later when counseling specific to paraplegia was available. So without any attempt on her part to make amends, the dysfunctional games would simply have continued unabated. I wasn't helping Johnnie by continuing to play the game. I was reinforcing and enabling her dysfunctional behavior. I had to say, "It's over." I was no longer the Augustus Family Secret scapegoat. I was free at last!

I wonder whether being the favored child, the Son, was a blessing or a curse for Dean. It isn't fair to judge him by the standards of today. All he had to base his actions on were the roles of his parents and grandparents and relatives and friends at that particular time in history. His ideas about male-female relationships were formed during a time when women were not considered equal to men.

I couldn't face asking him about Mother's murder attempts and he couldn't face telling me about what had happened in the Colorado kitchen. I understand the difficulty of bringing family secrets out of hiding. It isn't easy and I don't blame him. His mother placed him in a no-win situation.

The lesson for me with my brother is that life isn't always fair, but life is what you make it. Dean could have just given up and wallowed in his paralysis after his accident. But he had a positive attitude and met the challenge head on. I am proud to be the little sister of Dean Edward Augustus.

1. Dean Augustus as a child in Colorado. 2. Dean Augustus, high school graduation picture. 3. Dean as a young man. 4. Left: Cousin Dora Jean DeVoss, Dean, Juanita (Johnnie), Norma. 5. Dean and Johnnie. 6. Johnnie and Dean at home. 7. Left: Murray Dean, Douglas, Dennis Edward. 8. Murray Dean, Dennis, Doug. 9. Logging operation in Klamath Falls. 10. Dean at Good Samaritan Hospital after logging accident. 11. Dean with grandson Jason. 12. Dean worked after accident.

CHAPTER FIVE
MARJORY - MY SISTER MY SAVIOR

My sister, Marjory Yvonne Augustus, was born two years after her brother, Dean, in Blanca, Colorado. Della's family model was typical of life in the early 1900s. Daughters were just worthless girls who could do nothing right. She was first in line to be belittled and humiliated by her mother because she was a daughter, just a worthless girl and a reminder of her own childhood and the injustice she suffered simply because she was born female and was the oldest daughter.

Marjory, or Marge as most people called her, graduated from Blanca High School and excelled in mathematics—very much against the *norm* for girls in that era. She graduated from Blair Business College in Colorado Springs a year later earning a Life Scholarship Degree. Marge was tiny: only 5' 4" and never weighted more than 105 pounds, but she approached life with the courage of a linebacker.

Marge, was the only loving, caring mother figure in my life. She was sixteen when I was born and I had two wonderful years of her doting love and affection before she left to attend business school. Nobody in my family talked much about our lives in Colorado. Maybe they were glad to put it behind them and start over in Oregon.

The memories I have of Marge begin in Oregon. She always had a smile for me, and seeing her laughing at the wonders of life gave me hope that I could have a better life. Marge was generous and loving. Mother never dared to hit me when Marge was visiting.

She let me use her bicycle with no instructions or restrictions and she gave it to me when she moved to California. I don't think she ever knew that my father ran over her beloved bicycle with his Ford panel truck. He told me never to ride across the bridge that arched over the Klamath River not far from our house. He knew I had disobeyed him when I arrived home dripping wet from sliding on the gravel on the other side of the bridge and into the river. I couldn't talk my way out of that mess.

Marge had faith in herself as a woman of value and thought life was an adventure to be explored and enjoyed to the fullest. She trusted happiness. After moving to Klamath Falls in 1936 with her brother, Dean, Marge worked at Montgomery Ward in the accounting department. It was there that she met the love of her life, O. C. Davies. He was the store manager and had been separated from his wife for several years. However, she was a Roman Catholic and refused to agree to a divorce. Laws at that time prevented one partner in a marriage from divorcing the other without their permission. Marge and O. C. were engaged for fourteen years and were friends for life.

Marge and O. C. moved to California when I was fourteen. I was forlorn to put it mildly. They lived separately in the San Francisco Bay area. In those days it was unheard of for men and women who were not married to live in the same house. If they could fast forward to today they would simply live together. I remember wonderful trips to the redwood forests and Yosemite National Park with Marge and O. C.

Marge never considered marriage to anyone except O. C. She was not afraid to wait hoping that his wife would tire of her non-marriage after decades of not having a live-in husband. Being a single woman in a society based on married couples was a challenge. Women who weren't married made people nervous; there had to be something wrong with them. Were they man haters? Were they lesbians? They were different.

Moving to a large cosmopolitan city gave Marge opportunities she would not have had in Klamath Falls. She first lived in Sunnyvale, in the southern San Francisco Bay area, and worked for Westinghouse Electric Corporation in the accounting department. Westinghouse manufactured electrical transformers. It was the beginning of the post war industrial expansion into the orchards and farms of Santa Clara County, which would become known years later as Silicon Valley.

The electrical industry seemed to be a good fit for Marge, so it was a natural move after three years at Westinghouse for her to seek work at Pacific Gas & Electric (PG&E) in the accounting department. She was hired, moved to Berkeley across the bay, and worked for PG&E in San Francisco for thirty-two years.

At the time, she expected to eventually be a married woman. When that didn't happen she still made a good life for herself. She had friends, succeeded in the business world, and earned enough money to buy jade jewelry, Baccarat crystal, and designer clothes. She loved to travel, and attend cultural events in Berkeley and San Francisco.

I spent several weeks with my sister every summer after my tenth birthday traveling by train to Berkeley. Marge didn't flinch when I told her once that I was the only passenger in the rail car who wasn't an Italian prisoner of war. The conductor checked on me frequently, but I didn't have any complaints.

The men kept me supplied with candy and cookies. They didn't seem unhappy about being prisoners and sang with great enthusiasm for the entire trip, through the Siskiyou Mountains in northern California, the Sacramento Valley, and into Oakland, where my journey ended. The singing Italians were going to San Francisco—the end of the line. It was a wonderful experience. I always remember it with a smile. Marge knew I could handle about anything. I was her sister. I was always someone special.

Now I realize how thoughtfully she planned my visits. She introduced me to the cultural and entertainment offerings of the big city and sent me home with expensive clothes from fancy stores.

Marge had confidence in her little sister. On the days she was working she wrote directions for me about which bus to take to get me where I wanted to go. In those days, it was safe for a ten-year old or a young teenager to explore the 'City,' i.e., San Francisco, alone.

I always explored the University of California Berkeley campus first to see if there were any changes from the previous year. And then I'd head for San Francisco. The tall buildings were of course a wonder to the country girl from Southern Oregon. But I never ventured inside those towering buildings so my hidden falling-off-the-counter memories stored deep in my psyche were not awakened.

I spent the most time, year after year, in Golden Gate Park. I loved the serenity of the Japanese Garden and the creek flowing under the arching moon bridge. In later years, I looked forward to seeing the man that would tap his cane on the bamboo fence to call the squirrels. They came scurrying happily from every direction to devour the peanuts he brought them. I think of him when I feed the squirrel that visits me almost every day. Marge trusted me and introduced me to the wonders of the City of San Francisco.

Marge was a wonderful role model for me. She showed me that there was more to life than the violence that defined my relationship with my mother.

Marge lived in Berkeley on Durant Avenue for thirty-two years. When the University of California bought her apartment building for a parking lot she moved closer to Shattuck Avenue. That neighborhood made the network news when it was announced as one of the areas where the Symbionese Liberation Army had held Patty Hearst captive. Marjory and her neighbors had wondered what was going on in an apartment directly across the street from their building because the windows had been covered with sheets at one time. "Oh, if we had only known" was the general feeling when they learned that Patty Hearst had been their neighbor.

The second time Marge's neighborhood made the nightly network news was when soldiers with bayonets drawn protected the businesses on Shattuck Avenue from rampaging University of California students. They were protesting the Vietnam War. Marge was in Oregon with us and we were relieved to know she hadn't had to deal with what looked like a war zone as she was trying to get home after work. That was an aberration for the usually calm Durant/Shattuck neighborhood.

Being just a half block west of Shattuck Avenue, Marge was closer to shopping and recreational opportunities with a theatre, grocery store, and a jewelry store owned by a Chinese family. Their store featured jade jewelry and ivory artifacts. She bought some of each. They oversaw the construction of two ten feet tall teak cupboards finished with black lacquer, which she used as elegant storage for her treasures and her clothes. Marjory enjoyed the finer things in life and especially appreciated anything Asian.

By having long-time employment with a large company and building a business relationship with the Chinese jeweler she obtained defacto credit even though the laws of the land had not yet approved such business ventures. Marge was a good customer and I am the benefactor of her good taste. Her "finds" are proudly displayed in every room of my home.

Marge was promoted many times during the thirty-two years she worked at Pacific Gas and Electric, but never to top management positions. It was her responsibility, however, to always train the men who would then become her manager. Marge was stoic about hitting the glass ceiling for women long before this reality was first recognized and challenged. Her attitude was life isn't always fair. She was a country girl, happy to have done well in the big city. She retired from PG&E after working there happily for thirty-two years.

I wish I had asked Marge why she didn't pursue a four-year university degree, since the University of California campus at Berkeley was across the street from her apartment. It might have made a difference in her career.

She had three successful years at Westinghouse before transferring to PG&E, but getting hired by major corporations before any Supreme Court decisions or Congressional actions or the national women's rights discussions says a lot about Marjory. And it says a lot about Westinghouse and PG&E. She had business school credentials as well as a solid work history as an accountant and neither company made gender an issue.

For efficiency in getting dressed for work early in the morning, all of Marge's clothes were either black or white with only an occasional red accessory. She was a perfectionist and I watched in awe as she ripped apart Christian Dior suits and sewed them back together by hand with the tiniest stitches you can imagine. It wasn't that they needed alteration to fit her size four body. My sister from Blanca, Colorado was not satisfied with the quality of her House of Dior garments.

Her shoes were lined up in a row in the closet like soldiers at attention. Nobody was allowed to touch them. That was the only thing she fussed about with her little sister. I had to be careful that adding my shoes to the lineup didn't get hers out of place. I didn't understand then the significance of those shoes.

After our mother had a stroke, she must have done some soul searching about her life and Marjory's and my life. Marge came to visit her and she expressed concern about the sixteen-year age difference between Marjory and me. From her Village Nursing Home bed, she made us promise that we would take a long trip to get to know each other better. We kept our promise. We toured Southeast Asia for three weeks, visiting Japan, Taiwan, Philippines, Singapore, Thailand, and Hong Kong.

Our trip was booked through the PG&E travel service for employees, which was a huge advantage. The size of our group was small, only sixteen people. We had opportunities larger groups couldn't even dream of such as visiting a Tokyo school principal's home where we had tea and cookies and learned about the importance of energy conservation. It was not customary to heat an entire room. Instead, we sat at low-skirted tables outfitted with a heat lamp to keep us warm. I think of the principal and his wife when I wrap my legs with a throw instead of turning up the heat on a cold night.

Marge fell in love with the Nara Deer Park in Japan. She wanted to take every deer back to Berkeley, but settled for six bronze replicas. Three now live happily on a ledge in my great room surrounded by pine trees and silk screens as reminders of my sister and mentor.

We enjoyed the museums, galleries, and gardens in Taiwan. We didn't know quite what to think about Filipino newspaper headlines that warned, "Plot to stir up chaos and violence. STAY INDOORS. MANILA ALERT." Military escorts with machine guns at the ready were with us everywhere we went in the Philippines, but we didn't let that ruin our visit. In Singapore, I learned that if you're told a spice is too hot for beginners, believe it, even if you're eating at the Raffles Hotel. I was impressed with their wise use of land with businesses, housing, and daycare in the same high-rise building. In Thailand, we marveled at women dressed in beautiful striped Thai silk skirts and jackets working on road-building crews. In Hong Kong, we were amazed at the agility of Chinese women; all dressed in black, and hoisting baskets half as large as they were onto bamboo poles and carrying them to the market to shop for their families.

As we learned about these magical countries and talked until late in the night we learned about each other. I am grateful for that special time we had together.

In January, four years after our Asian tour, Marjory Yvonne Augustus died of a cerebral hemorrhage from a ruptured aneurysm shortly after she retired from PG&E. She was washing her beloved embroidered sheets by hand in her kitchen sink when she died. The running water overflowed into the lobby of her apartment building alerting the manager that all was not well with Miss Augustus. The county coroner left a message on our family answering machine to call him. There is only one reason to call a coroner and I suppose there is no other way to handle a sudden death, but it was a brutalizing experience.

Marge had looked forward to traveling extensively when she retired and she would have had access to the services of the PG&E employee travel department. I don't think she was pleased about her time on this Earth ending before she fulfilled that dream. For the rest of that terrible day all the electronic devices in my home office: the answering machine, electric typewriter, printer, and telephone were dead. My computer screen was filled with digital gibberish. Marge wanted me to know that she was not happy. She still had things to do and people and places to see.

We had to empty her apartment and my heart almost stopped when I opened the door to her basement storeroom. It was filled with stack after stack of shoeboxes. Inside each of the several hundred boxes was a pair of shoes wrapped neatly in white tissue paper with a sales receipt to remember the year they were purchased and the price paid for the shoes. My son, Skip, remembers seeing a sales receipt dated in the 1940s.

I cried for my sister who, as a young girl during the Great Depression, had to wear worn-out shoes tied with rope to keep the soles from falling off because her mother would buy shoes only for her brother. The message from her mother was clear. Girls in general and Marjory specifically had no value. It obviously haunted her until the day she died.

Every year before school started, Marjory would send me a box of clothes and shoes for which I was always grateful. It was clear to me after seeing her storeroom why she had been so faithful about seeing that I had new clothes. She was afraid our mother would make me go to school in the equivalent of worn-out shoes tied with rope.

As I looked through her clothes closets I was surprised to find a brown Christian Dior dress among the black and white dresses and suits she always wore. Her friend told me that it was her latest wardrobe addition. I chose the daring brown dress for her burial. My sister from Blanca, Colorado deserved to be buried in a Christian Dior frock.

When we arrived at her apartment, all the money in Marge's purse was gone except for some coins. So when I couldn't find her jade ring I thought someone had stolen it as well as her money. The ring had a history. I bought a jade ring first. Then she bought one. Her ring was larger and the jade was better quality than mine. The setting, hand made by her Chinese jeweler friend, was magnificent. Marge wasn't going to be outdone by her little sister. I was upset when I couldn't find her prized ring, but nothing else except money seemed to be missing. Her zebra rugs and pillows, her Baccarat vases and crystal balls, her sterling silver, and her ivory figurines would have been obvious and safe targets for an early morning theft.

I was responsible for arranging her funeral so I couldn't spend time or effort worrying about or searching for the ring. We buried Marjory Yvonne Augustus high in the Berkeley hills. Her grave overlooks the San Francisco Bay and is located at the edge of a section for people of Chinese descent. She loved anything Asian so I had her head stone engraved in Chinese as well as English.

After the funeral I called a Portland psychic, Maxine Shaw, to see if she could help us find the jade ring. She worked with police departments around the country and had a good reputation. She said it was in the pocket of a brown dress. Since Marge had only one brown dress and I had chosen that dress for her burial, I said good-bye to the ring. I was not going to dig up my sister to look for a ring, not even a jade ring bigger and better than mine.

Several months later, however, I was going through a box of Marge's belongings and was amazed to find the lost ring. It was in a box I had already searched. I called Maxine Shaw and told her about my discovery. She said it had been "transformed from the brown dress to the box because Marge was ready for me to have it." I thought, "OK," but I was grateful to have it. Now Marge's ring never leaves my finger except for cleaning. I don't want it "transforming" again.

I donated all of Marjory's shoes to a community theatre group and I hope they danced happily ever after. Most of her size four designer clothes went to my friend, Martha Bergman. She said the quality and style of Marge's carefully chosen wardrobe increased her confidence and she moved from Portland to New York City expanding her successful career in television production. In a twist of fate, Martha then met a man from Portland who was on a business trip to New York, and they are happily married living in Portland. She took on a new career organizing a Toyota style production line for her husband's long-standing family business of producing oil paints for artists around the world. I am more than a little certain that Marge is very pleased about being part of Martha's success and happiness.

I wish Marjory and I had talked more about the shoes. The storeroom was clear evidence that neither her mother nor her brother ever talked to Marjory about the humiliation she endured always being in the shadow of the favored son. The wounds inflicted by her mother stayed open and bleeding until the day she died.

Marge had the ability, confidence, and courage to work in a field dominated by men. She always had a Plan B if there was a problem with Plan A. That is just one lesson I learned from my big sister, my savior and mentor. It is a sobering experience to bury the last member of your birth family. There is nobody left but me as the keeper of our memories, and nobody to answer the questions I should have asked decades ago.

Did Mother ever regret always favoring her son? Why didn't she apologize to Marge? Was she punishing Marge for foiling her murder attempts?

I loved my sister and she loved me. That's all that matters. I am proud to the little sister of Marjory Yvonne Augustus.

1. Marjory Augustus in San Diego. 2. O. C. Davies, Marge's fiancé for 14 years. 3. O. C. and Marge.
4. Marge loved to knit. 5. Marge at home in Berkeley. 6. Marge loved her ivory figurines.
7. Marge celebrating Christmas. 8. Monaco Theatre Restaurant in San Francisco.
9. O. C., Marge and Johnnie and Dean. 10. Off to tour SE Asia.

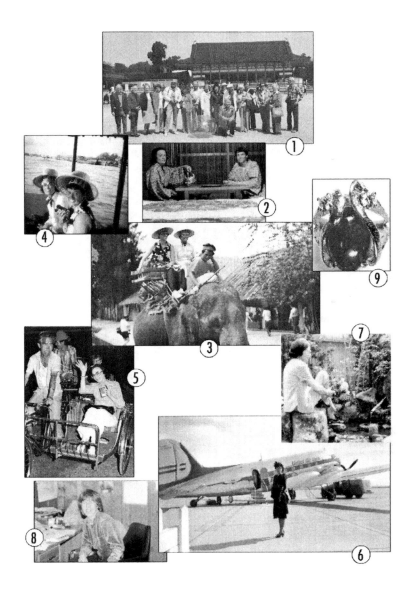

1. SE Asian PG&E tour group. 2. Tea in Japan. 3. Riding elephants in Thailand. 4. Thailand river cruise. 5. Marge in rickshaw. 6. Coming home to Klamath Falls. 7. Marge in McRobert Japanese Garden. 8. Martha Bergman inherited Marge's size four clothes. 9. Marge's bigger and better Jade ring.

CHAPTER SIX

OFF TO THE BIG CITY

Career options for women when I graduated from high school were limited to teaching, nursing, and home economics. Only rarely did a woman venture into other fields. I developed an interest in medicine because of my father's tuberculosis and my brother's paraplegia. With graduation approaching, I investigated the various nursing schools in Oregon. Going to medical school never occurred to me.

A scholarship from a women's service club, Soroptimist International of Klamath Falls paid my tuition as well as room and board at the school with the highest rating in the state from the National League of Nursing—Providence Hospital School of Nursing in Portland. So off I went filled with the over confidence typical of eighteen year olds who think they know all the answers before they know the questions.

Like all nursing schools in those days students were unmarried women. They lived in housing on the hospital grounds and split their time evenly between the classroom and working in various hospital departments four hours a day, five days a week at no cost to the hospital. This kept the cost of care low for patients and tuition low for students. The quid pro quo was good for everyone. Nurses were very much handmaidens to physicians. When a doctor (male) came into a room, the nurses (female) had to stand to show respect. I should have known then that the nursing field was not going to work for me long-term.

It was at Providence School of Nursing that I first took a stand against the establishment when it limited choices. Sister Elizabeth Ann was director and we lived by her rules every minute of every day. Students were limited to wearing only white sweaters with their uniforms. But students wanted a choice of colors.

Some finally rebelled and brought the issue to the Student Council, of which I was a member. We suggested the issue be resolved with a vote by the student-body. Sister agreed but when the votes were tallied and the colored sweaters won, she reneged. She basically told us that our vote didn't count and while it was an interesting experiment but the white-sweater rule would continue.

I disagreed with her. Since she had approved the election, she should honor the outcome even though she didn't like it. That's democracy. Others on the Council agreed, and she backed down. We were pleased but amazed that the very serious nun gave up so easily. These days, when voters speak and the politicians don't listen, I think of that election. To me it's clear-cut: It's simply a pink-sweater moment.

Sister Elizabeth Ann had another "Oh, Miss Augustus!" moment one day as she was passing out our mail. Although we each had mailboxes, we had to gather in the lobby so she could give us our mail, piece by piece. One day she read the headlines of my *Herald & News* paper from Klamath Falls: *Baldy Band Members Arrested on Drug Charges.* "Oh, dear, Miss Augustus!" she said clearly troubled by the story. The big band musicians who came to town apparently brought more than their musical instruments. They also brought drugs, which were new to Oregon at the time. I was a trial to poor Sister Elizabeth Ann.

I met Marshall Brown, M.D. at Providence Hospital. While another student and her mother thought he was a good catch, I had misgivings when he asked me for a date. I didn't trust doctors. One delayed the diagnosis of my father's tuberculosis so long it killed him. Another lacked the training and skill to perform spinal cord surgery on my brother and did it anyway. There was also something about him that just didn't ring true to me. My Montana Distrust factor was giving me warning signals.

I suspect it was my lack of interest that made me a challenge and after a year I ignored my inner warnings and began dating him. Our dysfunctional traits fit like precisely tooled gears. I repeated my past as wife instead of daughter and the relationship was doomed before it began. The marriage was a retreat back into the hell that was my childhood and yet again, my very life was at stake.

Later I learned our relationship had an additional obstacle. A marriage to Marshall automatically included a third person—his mother. To be precise, Marshall's haunting recollections of being sexual abused by his mother when she was in between husbands. She had four.

We were married in October 1953 at St. Ignatius Church in Portland. By January 1954, I was pregnant and nursing school had to be put on hold. I thought I could finish my nursing education at any Catholic Hospital School of Nursing, but that was not the case and it was many years later when I could finish that chapter of my life.

Marshall then decided he wanted to be a psychiatrist. He was accepted at the Menninger Clinic in Topeka, Kansas. So we headed to Kansas with a detour to visit his mother in Virginia, Minnesota.

I should have suspected then that something was awry between Marshall and his mother. She called me a "pregnant cow" and chased me out of the house with a butcher knife. Marshall expected me to go back inside as if nothing unusual had happened. His mother was a crazed woman and she obviously wanted me dead. No way was I going back in that house. I stood in the middle of the street until he collected our belongings.

I didn't understand then that his mother saw me as a competitor. My life had been strange, but not that strange. We left immediately for Kansas.

Our first son, Skip, was born in Topeka, Kansas. But after six months, Marshall decided he didn't want to be a psychiatrist and we moved back to Oregon.

We opened a medical office in Gresham with Marshall practicing general medicine. I got the office up and running and worked without pay full-time for a year and filled in for vacations and on Saturdays for five years also without pay.

The same week the office opened for business, Marshall began psychoanalysis with a Freudian psychiatrist who wanted me to see another Freudian psychiatrist since he didn't work with couples. I was told that if I would be "more passive, our marriage would succeed." He also said my short pixie hairstyle was "hostile" and never once looked me straight in the eye. I told him, "I don't want to end up like you," walked out the door, and never went back. No more Freudian psychobabble for me.

The Freudian view of an appropriate role for women, particularly married women pleased Marshall. If I wasn't appropriately passive, I heard about it. Nag, nag, nag.

Or if I had any activities that weren't strictly home related it was nag, nag, nag. I played golf with two women friends every Friday at noon, rain or shine, and I had to pay the piper just as I had with my mother—bad times followed good times. No act of fun went unpunished. My second activity was monthly meetings of the Terra Maids Garden Club. I was used to plant material hardy enough to withstand the snow and freezing blizzards of Southern Oregon and I wanted to learn what flourished in the mild climate of the Willamette Valley. That too was unacceptable. So it was nag, nag, and more nag.

Marshall charged that I was neglecting Skip and not doing the housework to his standards. I never left Skip with a baby sitter two days in a row and the house was not a mess. At first I did the house cleaning, kept up a sizeable yard, took care of our children, and all the other "chores" that went with being a housewife. Later we hired a landscape company to do the yard. But help with the two-story Colonial was out of the question and getting an automatic dishwasher was not seen as appropriate until much later.

Six years after we married, Marshall told me he was a victim of his mother's sexual abuse when she was in between husbands. Later I understood that his mother's incestuous relationship defined and dominated his sex life.

Alcohol made everything worse. His nightly wine made him just plain mean and ruined holiday celebrations just as my father had done year after year.

Criticism and fighting act as distancing mechanisms to decrease the uneasiness felt from being close to an "official" partner.

"Official" sex partners, i.e., a willing wife, especially one near the same age, turns on the reminder incest tapes and brings back memories and pain of being sexual assaulted by mothers and/or fathers—a marriage partner feels too emotionally similar to the offending parent.

Promiscuity, however, does not turn on those tortuous tapes and is frequently the solution chosen by incest victims to avoid "official" partners. That was the solution Marshall chose and he must have thought he had died and gone to heaven when Gresham's first hospital opened.

I didn't know then that the first Gresham Hospital was known as Peyton Place and had a reputation as a place for reckless sexual encounters in empty patient rooms where some doctors, administrators, and nurses played house. I knew Marshall was gone more often in the evenings but I didn't care. In fact, I was relieved to be rid of him.

However, having been raised as an only child, I wanted Skip to have a brother or a sister. We adopted a beautiful boy, only three days old, and named him Gregory John. Then with the help of Dr. Ivan Langley's weekly medical treatments, a third son, Timothy, rounded out our family.

Three months into my second pregnancy, a car hit me when I was crossing a street. The driver said the sun blinded him and he didn't see me. Our friend Leo Smothers happened to be in the area and saw me spiraling through the air and landing in the middle of the intersection. He rushed to help and it was good to have a friend concerned about me.

Somebody telephoned Marshall. The intersection where I was lying in the middle of the street was just a block from his office. He did come to see what happened, but didn't examine me, or inquire in I have any particular pain. He made it clear that I was not a priority. If I got myself into this mess, I could get myself out of it. He said, "I have an office full of people."

My physician husband left without instructing anyone on what to do with his wife who had disrupted his schedule. I don't know who called the ambulance that took me to the hospital emergency room where doctors assured me that I had no broken bones. I don't remember how I got home.

A few weeks later, however, I developed excruciating pain in the right flank of my lower back. Exploratory surgery showed that an ovarian vein, swollen to the size of a garden hose, had blocked my kidney. Since that ovary was the only one to support the pregnancy, and I was determined to have that baby, doctors inserted a catheter into my kidney as a temporary drain. As my health deteriorated from continuous kidney infections caused by a super-bug strain of pseudomonas bacteria, I was in and out of the hospital every two weeks. With temperatures reaching 106 degrees, I floated out of my body watching the nurses' pack me in ice from a cooler observation post—the ceiling.

Marshall finally bought an electric, automatic dishwasher to help the woman hired to care for the household and children because of my illness.

Marshall tested positive for a virulent strain of pseudomonas bacteria probably contracted from one of his sex partners at his office, one or both of my "friends" who had affairs with him, or the Gresham Hospital. He then passed it on to me. So it was Marshall's sexual antics that caused my ongoing kidney infections because that particular strain of pseudomonas seemed immune to antibiotics. I was never off antibiotics more than two weeks at a time for five years.

Desperate doctors then prescribed a urinary antiseptic called Mandelamine. I was so grateful to be pseudomonas-free that I didn't question why it was so effective.

Sixteen years later, I learned Mandelamine worked because it created formaldehyde and by then I was sensitive not only to formaldehyde but all chemicals, i.e., the world.

When I stopped dosing myself with formaldehyde four times a day, I had three weeks of hellish withdrawal symptoms: terrible nausea, vomiting, and diarrhea;

blotches of subcutaneous bleeding all over my body, and nuclear level itching so bad that my second and forever husband, Chet, tied mittens on my hands when I slept so I couldn't scratch myself until I bled.

Chet took care of me and never complained. It was his suggestion that we try acupuncture and the results were miraculous. The itching stopped after the second treatment and gradually all the symptoms except chemical sensitivities stopped as well. Acupuncture helped heal my formaldehyde-ravaged immune system.

John Green, M.D. was only one physician in the entire state who acknowledged that chemical sensitivities were real, and the Oregon Medical Association (OMA) harassed him. How dare he help those of us who didn't quite fit the official playbook of the OMA!

Blood tests showed my white blood cells, particularly the T cells were in trouble, and my immune system was near collapse. That explained my continued lack of energy. Dr. Green said I was very close to having AIDS caused by sixteen years of formaldehyde poisoning.

He diagnosed thirty-two chemical sensitivities and provided me with antigens to counteract them. I continued the 10,000 milligrams of Vitamin C daily I had taken for years and a handful of other supplements prescribed earlier by Dr. Bly with some added by Dr. Green and a sugar-free diet. Slowly but surely my immune system healed and my energy returned. I still follow their advice and have a cupboard full of supplements prescribed by various doctors overtime.

I felt like the canary in the coal mine. Now "Environmental, Integrative, and Ecological" medical practitioners are easier to find.

Over the past four decades, this disorder caused by Marshall's killer strain of pseudomonas bacteria has cost us tens and tens of thousands of dollars starting with medical bills not covered by insurance, rehabilitating our house: sealing all the walls to prevent the off-gassing of formaldehyde from the wall board, replacing carpets, drapes, and furniture made of synthetic petroleum based products that contained formaldehyde. Expensive air filters were added to almost every room as well as the furnace.

Chet stripped an old Mustang of all vinyl so the doors and dashboard were down to metal. He sealed the fabric-covered seats with the same masonry sealer we used on the walls, took out the carpeting, and found an air filter that could be plugged into the cigarette lighter. I got strange looks and questions from gas station attendants. I admitted that my stripped down Mustang didn't have much market appeal but assured them that it was perfect for me.

I had to time my travel to avoid rush hour traffic with delays that caused air pollution. If we traveled by air, I wore expensive masks. In hotels, I had to take an air filter, sheets, towels, and pillowcases that were chemical-free and safe or I would suffer.

But newer hotels with walls and carpets loaded with formaldehyde were problematic. We had to leave a new hotel in Santa Monica in the middle of the night for an older motel in Marina del Ray after spending an hour on the phone searching for an older facility. Living with chemical sensitivities was expensive, nerve wracking, time consuming, and continues to be expensive because some of the treatments that help the most are still not covered by insurance. There are some limitations to my immune system to this day. I cannot attend concerts or plays or symphonies in buildings without high ceilings and good air filtration systems. It seems that fans of these musical events are also fans of cologne and perfume—lots of it and much too much for me since it breaks down into formaldehyde and ozone.

Chemical sensitivities are yet one more health issue, one that changed my life forever, caused by Marshall's promiscuous sexual behavior.

Marshall's response to my reoccurring kidney infections, which he caused was anger. I was also in constant pain from the wire sutures pulling against my enlarging abdomen and a damaged nerve that had been crushed by the rib spreader used during my surgery. His daily message was that I was causing too much trouble and that my illness interfered with his life.

The reality is that spending time with me at the hospital meant he had less time to spend with his lady friends. He showed no concern for me, or our baby. He told me that my four-foot long surgical scar that spiraled from just under my shoulder blade down to my hip bone and across my abdomen with a protruding catheter that drained my obstructed kidney was quote unquote "repulsive." I said, "Go to hell you monster," and I promised myself I was going to divorce him as soon as I was physically able to do so.

Twenty years later I learned Marshall had asked Dr. Ivan Langley to abort our baby. Dr. Langley told him that if I was willing to endure the agony I was going through to have a healthy baby, it was my right to have that opportunity. He told Marshall that the only way he would consider abortion is if I asked him to end the pregnancy. I am a pro-choice feminist. It isn't that I considered abortion and rejected it as an option. It was never even on my radar screen. I wanted that baby.

In mid-September, the kidney started draining, which meant it was not the pregnancy that caused the ovarian vein to swell like a garden hose blocking my kidney. It was the pesky car that threw me twirling into the air before I crashed to the street. On October 9th, I delivered a healthy five and a half pound son. He was beautiful and worth every minute of the pain I went through to bring him into the world. Being the youngest, Tim always wanted to be bigger than his brothers. He topped off at six feet-three inches and is the tallest of the guys.

I hemorrhaged a week after Tim was born. At 7:00 PM it was just a blood clot and I called Dr. Langley who said to keep him informed of any changes. At 2:00 AM, I stood up to get out of bed and after the time it took to walk the thirty feet to the bathroom blood gushed everywhere.

Marshall would have let me bleed to death waiting for an ambulance because he didn't want to get blood all over his new car. Neither Marshall nor I had called Dr. Langley, but somehow he knew I was in trouble and he arrived at our house before the ambulance. He pounded on the door, ran up the stairs, picked me up off the floor, and wrapped me in a blanket he grabbed from our bed. Then he carried me downstairs and took me to the hospital in his new Porsche. Dr. Langley was not concerned about the upholstery in his new Porsche being ruined by his bloody patient.

His understanding of my marital situation along with his willingness to confront a colleague and take action, his surgical skills, and four pints of blood saved my life. It is impossible to put into words the gratitude I feel for Dr. Langley's understanding, caring, and expertise.

My urologist, Dr. Charles Catlow, was also aware of my problems at home and lectured me that if I wanted to live to raise my children, I would have to make drastic choices about my marriage. It all crystallized when I collapsed on the floor with a high fever from a staph infection and Marshall refused to help me get back to bed and he refused to get help. I crawled back to bed from the bathroom, called Dr. Catlow, and then called for an ambulance to take me to the hospital.

Dr. Catlow refused to discharge me until I had hotel reservations in Hawaii. He wanted me out of town where I could think about my marriage problems and make the decision when, not if, I was going to file for divorce. Hawaii was a relatively short and easy flight, which was important since my health was shaky. Again, it's impossible to put into words the gratitude I feel to Dr.

Catlow. He also referred me to Carlton Reiter, the attorney who had represented his former wife, because he wanted me to have the best legal representation. After two weeks in Hawaii, I came home and filed for divorce. Marshall moved to an apartment.

Why didn't I end my marriage sooner? Divorce was an uncomfortable subject for a young woman in the early 1960s. I was a Providence School of Nursing Roman Catholic convert, living in a town of 3,500 people where everyone knew everything about everybody, and I was married to the town physician. There were no shelters and no safe houses. With three children, I couldn't pack my clothes in a cracker box and run away from home as I had in Colorado.

My health was another factor. I was in no shape for either fight or flight. Chronic kidney infections drain your energy and Marshall taunted me daily, "You're too sick to leave. Just try it, and you'll be back." I finally realized that it was the other way around. If I didn't leave, I would die.

I had to stay alive for my three sons, Skip, age seven, Greg, age two, and Tim, an infant. Skip and Greg hadn't been able to count on their mother being there for them for the past six months. They had also been victims of Marshall's constant criticism. We couldn't do anything right. Getting my sons out of that dysfunctional chaos to provide a stable environment for them was my top priority.

Those were the days before no-fault divorce, and Marshall filed a countersuit claiming I didn't have grounds for divorce. I called the police every time he broke into the house and when he was calling me on the phone every five minutes in the middle of the night. Lou Jones, the only police officer on duty, always came and he was helpful. He coached me on what to say to Marshall to attempt to get him to obey the restraining order that was supposed to keep me safe. He would also check on Marshall's whereabouts as a prevention measure. If Marshall's car was parked behind his office at 2:00 AM, Officer Jones knew he was calling me and made him go home to his apartment. Why he preferred his office as the official place to harass me is a mystery.

But no restraining order or calls from Officer Jones stopped Marshall's harassment. He broke into the house yet one more time in the middle of the night and came upstairs into my bedroom. In a state of terror my mind took me to someplace safe. It was dark. I could hear him telling me that he and the boys would be better off if I was dead. He said, "Do us a favor," and then threw three boxes of barbiturate sleeping pills on my bed—and then left.

I was in agonizing pain every minute of every day and night from muscle spasms caused by a nerve that was crushed during my kidney surgery. A neurosurgeon told me that if I would go back to my husband, my back would quit hurting, and he refused treatment. I walked into the bathroom saying to myself in total despair, "I will NEVER be rid of this pain. He will NEVER leave me alone and I will NEVER get away from him." I swallowed every Nembutal he had thrown at me and then walked back to the bedroom.

It wasn't dark. The lights were on. I remember calling Marshall and telling him to come and pick up the boys at ten the next morning, which was a Sunday because I wanted to sleep. Sometime during the night, he came back to the house and called an ambulance. Why he provided me with the means to kill myself and then called an ambulance is beyond my understanding unless it was to humiliate me, or as friends have pointed out, to prevent a charge of murder when police questioned where I got three boxes of Nembutal barbiturates. He directed the paramedics to take me to Holladay Park Hospital's crazy person section. I spent a week in the psychiatric wing and left determined that I was going to find a way to get Marshall Brown out of my life. FOREVER.

My orthopedist, Dr. Winfred Clarke resolved the pain in my back with surgery. He said the problem was not in my head. It was in my back.

Marshall, of course, now denies he refused to help me when I fainted and had to crawl back to bed. He denies he would have let me bleed to death rather than stain the upholstery in his new car. He denies he ever broke into the house.

When Judge Carl Dahl asked Marshall under oath if he really had done those things to me, he hung his head and admitted everything I said was true. Judge Dahl doubled the amount of alimony I had agreed to accept. My attorney, Carlton Reiter, referred me to his broker. And that was the beginning of my fascination with markets and investing which interest me to this day.

Marshall still insists I had no right to divorce him and he has convinced his second wife of his innocence. While the truth may hurt, I have learned the hard way that it's better to know the reality of a relationship instead of living in a dream world.

All I can say is that because our divorce in 1964 was before the days of "no fault" divorce, the public record of the daylong hearing (No. 269 565) is available for anyone to read. I've accepted my part in our dysfunctional relationship and moved on to a better life. I have succeeded in getting Marshall Brown out of my life FOREVER. That was my final escape from hell.

Women in those days never talked about sex or domestic violence. We acknowledged our pregnancies, but never the details of the events that brought them about. If there was emotional abuse or physical violence at home it became an unspoken family secret. So I never talked to any of my friends about the emotional abuse that was Marshall's at home specialty. That was my fifth family secret.

He belittled me constantly about anything and everything, but more so at our bridge and dinner groups, and any other time someone was around to watch him perform. He didn't miss a beat when I took a pincushion to our card games and suggested that he stick pins in it instead of me.

He ran his hand over the furniture to see if he could find some dust to complain about. He wore $500 suits and was furious if I bought a fresh pineapple. He also belittled our sons constantly. Nothing we did was good enough to satisfy him. He yelled at us. He would raise his hands as if to hit us and then pull back. Years later I learned that during one of his drunken break-ins, Marshall sexually assaulted our son. He has accepted responsibility for his actions and apologized.

I did talk to my priest, Father Meyer. He agreed that a divorce was inevitable with one caveat. He insisted that I apply for an annulment of the marriage. With three children, an annulment seemed more than a little hypocritical. I attended one hour of a couples weekend marriage retreat but left in disbelief when the priest assured everyone that their marriages would thrive if every night before bedtime, the wife would kneel before her husband and ask for his blessing. That was even worse than the Freudians.

Neither men nor women talked about childhood sexual abuse. Marshall was one of those men. There were no Twelve Step programs for either the victim or his or her spouse or partner in those days. I brought it up at a meeting with Marshall and his Freudian psychiatrist. After five years of analysis, Marshall had not yet told his doctor about this part of his past. The doctor acknowledged that incest would indeed affect our relationship but offered nothing further.

I was clueless about Marshall's promiscuity and the effect incest had on our relationship. Apparently Marshall's affairs with other women were anything but secret. I didn't find out until years later that Marshall had a reputation at Mt. Hood Medical Center for approaching nurses blatantly and inappropriately.

A friend told me he "hassled" her for several days to go with him to an out of town conference. She said, "No," and reminded him that she was married. He replied, "Why does that matter?" He made that statement in front of a group of nurses gathered in the hospital lobby who also knew he was dating a hospital employee and that she was quite pregnant.

I learned about Marshall's longstanding affairs after our divorce. I received a phone call about his sexual fervor for one of his office employees and Mr. Stefanek told me he was naming Marshall as the cause of his divorce from his wife who was a nurse at the Gresham Hospital. She probably thought he really cared about her. Again, the Stefanek divorce case is a public record for anyone to read.

Marshall's unresolved hatred of his mother almost got me killed yet one more time. Just weeks before our divorce was final Marshall attacked me when he brought the boys home from a weekend visit. I drove in after them, got out of the car, and he lunged at me, choked me, knocked me to the ground, and then kicked me. As he reached down to hit me again, I threw my car keys in his face. This distracted him enough that I was able to run across the field to Bennett and Carol Welsh's house. Marshall put the boys back in his car and drove away as if nothing had happened. The terror they must have felt haunts me even now—but if I hadn't followed the cardinal rule for domestic violence victims, stay safe and alive, they could have had a dead mother.

I went to the Gresham Hospital emergency room where the on-call physician, Dr. Alan Fisher, who was not part of the after hours "sextravaganzas," examined me. He ordered infrared photographs. The photos clearly showed bruises on my neck from his hands around my throat. They also showed bruises around the scar from the surgery six months earlier. That was where he kicked me. I kept those slides in my safe deposit box for years until I realized that I needed to destroy them and release the fear and memories they represented.

Within a week of that homicidal attack, Marshall told me it wasn't me he tried to kill. He said he saw "the face of his mother." He thought that excused what he had done and didn't understand why I was upset. The fact that he had violently attacked me was not something I should be concerned about at all. I told him "It would have been me you killed—not your mother." But there was little I could do to prevent future attacks.

In those days hospitals and doctors didn't have to report spousal violence to the police. If he had done the same thing to a stranger on the street, he would have gone to jail. My restraining order was meaningless. Violence against one's spouse was not nice but it was legal. Domestic violence was simply not a punishable offense in the 1960s. Women were still non-persons and could be beaten as a legal right of marriage.

For safety's sake, the Multnomah County Sheriff's Office was our pick-up and drop-off point for the boy's weekend visits for several years until we graduated to the Safeway parking lot.

I did succeed in getting Marshall Brown out of my life FOREVER. I have spoken to him only three times, twice when our sons were going to have surgery, and once at the wedding of another son.

Marshall still thinks I had no right to divorce him. To avoid accepting any responsibility for his actions, he blames everyone except the man he sees in the mirror. For example, he claims that Chet tried to kill him by loosening a lug on a wheel of his car. The fact is that it is much more likely that he did it himself as a way to get rid of me. His other attempts to kill me by neglect had failed but his attitude had not changed.

I remember it so vividly because he tried to get me to trade cars with him because one wheel was wobbling and he said it wasn't safe for him to drive it to the hospital. I just laughed—I was on my way to Salem, fifty miles away because my mother had just had surgery to remove a ruptured appendix. I asked him why it made any sense for me to drive his wobbly-wheeled car a hundred miles to Salem and back if it wasn't safe for him to drive it three miles to the hospital? I left him standing in the driveway.

The wounds inflicted Marshall's mother have not healed. I've moved on to a better life. I conquered my family secret demons and accepted my role in my unfortunate relationship with Marshall Brown.

My sister and I chose men who were not available. Hers was unable to get a divorce to marry, and mine was raw with wounds inflicted by his mother. Our choices reflected our own problems with trust and intimacy that we learned from our parents. It was not easy to replace the need for distance and protection with a healthier approach to relationships. But as my mother used to say, "Sometimes you have to get deeper into a mess to get to something better." She was right. I went from hell and back and I survived and thrived!

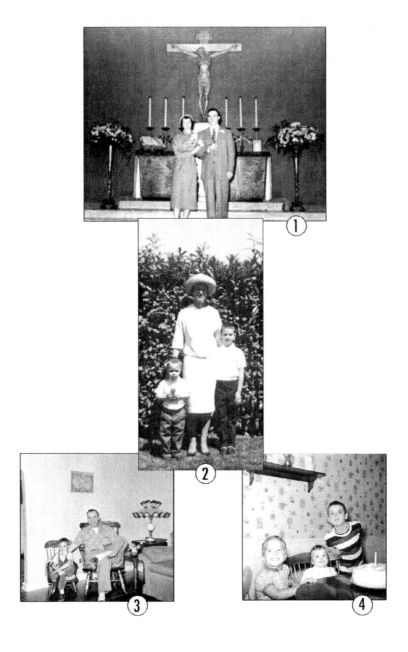

1. Gussie and Marshall Brown married at St. Ignatius Church. 2. Gussie with sons, Greg and Skip. 3. Marshall and Skip with matching chairs. 4. Celebrating Tim's first birthday.

CHAPTER SEVEN
OUT OF THE DARKNESS

To successfully end the cycle of abuse in my life, I had to understand the psychological demons that defined my relationships. Healing means being honest about your part in a relationship even if it means you have to relive old injuries.

I had to ask myself what happened to my confidence, assertiveness, and country girl training when I married a man like Marshall Brown. "He wore me down" is no excuse.

I made a vow to my family and myself when I left Holladay Park Hospital that the Augustus/DeVoss heritage of fear and abuse would end with me. I am not a psychologist, but from my decades long quest to understand the nuts and bolts of that heritage, and rise above it, I know it began with the simple act of refusing to be a victim.

I refused to allow Marshall Brown to destroy me with his perverted notions about the proper Freudian role of women and the shame and blame that accompanied that mindset. I learned slowly but surely that abuse and secrets gain power within a family only if they remain hidden.

The first part of the process meant I had to search for and listen to the tapes in my memory bank about the actions of my abusers, my responses to them, and how they had influenced my life, and my choices. Dr. Jack Butler, my very patient and non-Freudian counselor took me through that house of horrors at a pace that was safe to let the demons out of their cages one by one. Then I carefully examined each dysfunctional trait I had thought was normal, talked openly about it, and exchanged it for a more positive and less stressful approach to life.

One example is that now I immediately speak out if someone is distorting the facts about someone or something or is attempting to get me to do something or support something that doesn't feel right to me. My silence would be taken as agreement with whatever it was they wanted me to believe, say, or do. "That doesn't work for me," seems so simple, but if you have been trained from birth to never let anyone know exactly what you were feeling, it isn't easy. The alternative, staying in the abusive rut I had allowed myself to be put in was worse and was not acceptable.

Lots of reading self help books and participating in Adult Children of Alcoholic Parents and Al-Anon groups also helped me sort through what I wanted to keep and what I had to throw out.

Eventually, I came to understand that the attraction between Marshall Francis Brown and Norma Jean (Gussie) Augustus had at least two magnetic tapes buried deep in our subconscious memories that drew us together like moths attracted to a flame.

The first magnetic tape and the foundation on which I believe our attraction was based, was growing up in alcoholic homes with alcoholic parents. My father was an alcoholic; and Marshall's mother, father, and grandparents also had problems with alcohol. Our family models, which were based on dysfunctional behavior, were passed on to us.

I have come to believe that the second magnetic field of our attraction was created by our particular emotional responses to the alcoholic drama that ruled our lives as children.

From early childhood, my response to my mother's anger and brutality was fear. It felt like there was a fiery hole in my chest that sucked in the hatred Mother spewed at me day after day, hour after hour…"If it wasn't for you…" My reaction to the fear that I woke up with every morning and went to sleep with every night was to escape. I tried to get as far away from the source of that fear as I possibly could to stop the burning feeling in my chest.

How could Marshall not feel fear, distrust and anger with some role confusion and guilt added to the mix as he grew older and understood that having sex with your mother was not appropriate behavior? He was used as a sex toy in between her four husbands and then cast aside when a "real" man appeared.

Additionally, because Marshall didn't think his mother chasing me with a butcher knife was abnormal behavior; and he also didn't understand why I was upset when he choked me, punched me, and kicked me to the ground when he saw his mother's face instead of mine, it seems reasonable to assume that he must have experienced motherly rampages similar to those that I endured

We also shared at least one similar response to those rampages: escape. As an adult, he joined the Coast Guard and later after graduating from the prestigious University of Minnesota School of Medicine, he escaped from his abusive mother by fleeing half way across the country to Oregon instead of pursuing the numerous opportunities that would have been available to him in his home state of Minnesota.

Marshall's emotional responses to his particular genre of alcoholic drama were similar but not identical to mine because of his sexual abusive mother. I undoubtedly had an abundance of hidden residual fear from my mother's murder attempts but it was mostly her straightforward and continuous anger: "If it wasn't for you…." that preceded the floggings and beatings that I had to handle. My gigantic level of fear could have matched his more complex feelings of sexual abuse. Whatever it was, it seems clear that our matching tapes included "Growing Up With Alcoholic Parents" and "Emotional Responses to Alcoholic Parents." They were the magnets that drew us together and the fuel that fed the fire of our mutual attraction. It was what we called love.

Both our mothers stored their repressed anger in psychological reservoirs that occasionally overflowed onto us as outbursts of rage. These outbursts prevented our mothers from having an internal melt down or an out-in-the-open volcanic eruption. Their relief, however, was only temporary since their reservoirs always refilled to full capacity.

Their overflows and angry outbursts created and then filled our own reservoirs of Uncertainty, Distrust, and Fear. As children, we were safe targets for our parents' rage. We couldn't fight back.

I believe those outbursts actually relieved our uncertainty and fear temporarily because we didn't have to wonder about the When, Where, What, and Why of that particular blowup.

But it was not a permanent fix. Our reservoirs of Uncertainty, Distrust, and Fear began to refill as we immediately began to wonder When, Where, What, and Why would set off the next explosion. So the cycle continued as our psychological tapes recorded our stories about our abusive mothers.

This psychological phenomenon provided temporary emotional release for both mother and child in a dysfunctional game that never ended. It was a game with no winners and a game from which Marshall and I couldn't escape even as we fled across country and upstate from our abusers.

We were programmed to attract someone with the same psychological tapes who would know which buttons to push to activate the overflow safety valves in our psychic reservoirs. An argument or disagreement didn't have to be specific to our particular fear. It only had to provide the opportunity to empty our reservoirs of fear, distrust, and uncertainty. Marshall Brown and Norma Augustus were a perfect psychological and dysfunctional match. It had absolutely nothing to do with love.

Since Marshall and I weren't aware that these reservoirs, tapes, and buttons even existed, much less how they functioned, they were easily activated setting us up to continue playing the dysfunctional games we had learned from our mothers in our hellish childhoods.

After much healing, I was able to destroy those tapes and buttons by dragging them out of their dark hiding places where they lay waiting to torture me. They died of exposure to my new reality. With no "When, Where, What, and Why" concerns, my reservoirs of Uncertainty, Distrust, and Fear automatically emptied—never to be refilled.

I talked openly about my childhood experiences and my responses and reactions to my parent's dysfunctional and sometimes brutal actions. I talked about my abusive marriage and domestic violence.

I was the "blacked-out" woman on the KATU-TV newscast who admitted that I was once so desperately without hope that my ex-husband would stop breaking into the house in the middle of the night no matter how many times

I changed the locks, that I thought suicide was the only way to escape his violence.

I also told my story at churches and women's conference to bring domestic violence out in the open. My message to women was that emotional abuse and domestic violence was not acceptable and that all women had a right to be safe. I assured them that if they were in such a relationship that professional help was available, and that it was important not to hide their abuse from family and friends. I made it clear that I was not Super Woman and that if I could learn how to live without fear, they could learn how to live without fear.

I confessed that my silence about my abusive relationship was dishonest and that I had not wanted to admit to either myself or my friends and family that my marriage was less than perfect. That is why I am absolutely adamant about not allowing anyone to be dishonest about anything that relates to my friends, my family, or me. I refuse to play that game.

Another tape created in my subconscious by my mother's actions was the "bad times always follow good times" scenario that ruled our lives—the good times relieved her guilt but her hatred was stronger and always won that fight.

I conquered that tape on a ski trip to Vail, Colorado. My husband, Chet, insisted that I buy a new ski outfit and I chose one with a beautiful jacket with stripes of navy blue, dark chartreuse green, and two shades of orange.

Back in our condo, after a nice hot shower, I was reading in bed when suddenly a wave of free-floating anxiety started in my feet and streaked up by body finally landing in my chest like a bolt of lightning. I was terrified for just a moment until I realized that I was waiting for the axe to fall as the price I had to pay for the beautiful jacket. It was my "bad times always follow good times" tape and it was exposed in all its horror.

My reaction to this discovery was to sit up in bed and laugh—I finally got it! I dragged that "bad times always follows good times" demon tape out of my subconscious mind, and deactivated its pesky buttons. It shriveled up and died.

That beautiful striped jacket will always hang prominently on my wall as a trophy for winning a life without fear and a reminder of how I overcame my mother's hatred and brutality.

Marshall's ten-year long Freudian psychoanalysis and its celebration of passive women did not match my belief system. Since I had turned off my warning system that tried to tell me Marshall and I were not a healthy psychological match, it was absolutely critical that I find a way to reactivate it.

So I started paying attention to the reactions my body had to various people. When I was in the hospital during my pregnancy, it was focusing on whoever came to visit and also the nurses who were taking care of me. Later, it was anyone and everyone I talked to about anything. There was a tension in the center of my chest as if something was expanding that I felt with some people and not others.

Sometimes people were openly negative in a way that didn't lead to resolution of their concerns. That obviously meant trouble. Or if it was group conversation, the silence of someone not interacting alerted my internal warning system. Other times it felt as though the person was not telling the whole story. They seemed uneasy or the words they were saying didn't match their past actions.

For example, I would be willing to bet real money that a certain blonde nurse is the one who broke off a needle in my rear end and didn't bother to tell me that the syringe she had used was missing a needle. It still shows up on X-rays and I have to answer the question about how it got there. And then there was the two "friends," at least they called themselves "friends," who excoriated me for divorcing Dr. Brown when they had been two of his "lady" friends.

The tension I felt during these experiences was strong enough to eventually cause pain and I mentioned it to Dr. Paquet. He checked me with an earlier version of a fluoroscope and said my ribs and breastbone had been pulled apart by muscle spasms. He said it was stress related.

Because stress was a constant in my life at that time, it was no surprise that the pain disappeared as I healed physically and emotionally and learned to avoid the situations that caused the tension in the center of my chest.

A friend reminded me that my "warning" apparatus is in the same area as the heart chakra—or the Fourth Eye. I was in dire need of a Fourth Eye to sort through the dysfunctional nightmare I had been caught up in. I am grateful to have been able to work through my emotional pain so I could, over time lift myself out of the mire, make better choices, and move on to a better life. I survived and I thrived.

When I first sought professional help to tie up the loose ends I had unraveled about my upbringing and the relationships with my mother and first husband, I asked my family doctor for a referral to a psychiatrist who was not a Freudian. He said there was only one psychiatrist in Portland who he thought was safe for women to see and that was Dr. Jack Butler, mentioned at the beginning of this chapter.

I called Dr. Butler immediately for an appointment. His first action was to give me a widely used test called the Minnesota Multiphasic Instrument (MMPI). He laughed when he gave me the results of the test. I had been diagnosed as an "Aberrant Woman."

Because I wasn't passive and my confidence level was way too high, I didn't meet the American Psychological Association (APA) definition of a *normal* woman. The test was representative of the biased but socially accepted psychological norms for women in the 1960s.

I once pointed out the bias psychologists had against women by showing two charts from a book by Dr. Joyce Brothers during a speech I gave at a conference for and about women. The charts were side by side on one page. One listed the American Psychological Association's (APA) approved symptoms of depression. Next to it was the APA list of acceptable behavioral traits for women. They were identical! Dr. Joyce Brothers broke the silence on the bias against women in psychology and psychiatric circles. She was willing to risk her reputation and being scorned by her peers. We owe her a debt of gratitude for making this travesty public.

Treating women as inferior beings was not limited to psychology and psychiatry. In her book, *THE HIDDEN MALPRACTICE,* Gena Corea quoted an October 23, 1970 article in *MEDICAL WORLD NEWS,* which admitted that surgeons attending a cancer conference agreed they "rarely hesitated to remove an ovary but thought twice before removing a testicle." To sell drugs medical journal advertisements portrayed women as pathetic, but it was nothing that a magical pill couldn't cure. Women would then be drugged, but "happy housewives."

Fortunately, Dr. Paquet and Dr. Butler made me do it the hard way— absolutely no tranquilizers. I worked through my pain to gain a better understanding of how my mother's and Marshall's deadly abuse affected me and influenced the choices I made in life. Having a role model like my sister, Marjory, helped. The understanding and support of my second and forever husband, Chet, also helped. His acceptance neutralized the negative reactions I experienced from some people because I wasn't passive. I didn't meet the norm for women in the

1960s when I went back to school and worked in fields that were untraditional for women. Chet said if it was something I wanted to do, I should go for it.

The unconditional love I received from my father, brother, and sister also helped make up for Mother's hatred and abuse. Dean and Marge told stories about putting me in a red wagon and pulling it back and forth between them when I was an infant because there was no crib. It was my very good fortune that neither of them felt ashamed or angry about my birth.

As I mentioned earlier, psychological tests show that my confidence level is higher than average. Dr. Butler said this was likely the result of being the center of attention and feeling very loved during the first two years of my life.

So ironically, because of Mother's attempts to kill me, and my brother and sister staying home from school to protect me, I received a level of love and caring not possible in a household with several children where mothers can't spend all their time playing with one child. Dean and Marjory not only saved my life, their loving actions gave me a strong base of confidence that irritates some people but serves me well overall.

I now consider Mother's silence about my successes a tremendous blessing because it made me base my choices in life on my preferences only instead of whether they would please others. My life experiences prove there are lessons to be learned, and long-term benefits to be gained from even the most sinister circumstances.

While my mother thought I just a worthless girl, she also figured out that I had value as the family secret scapegoat. That scenario became clear to me over four decades, and only then could I begin to understand the destructive cycle that began before I was born.

Mother's anger about failing to kill her unwanted daughter and having to put up with her every day created a negative ambiance that spread like wildfire throughout our family. She had to be concerned that either Dean or Marjory would eventually tell me the truth. It was a whirlpool sucking me slowly but surely into the quicksand of uncertainty that ruled my life. Since I was the only one in our immediate family who didn't know about her attempts to end my life, I couldn't fight back.

Did Mother think her abusive behavior was normal? If she didn't see it as abnormal then she would have nothing to regret. But how could a mother possibly think her repeated attempts to murder her daughter were justified? Did she think her actions were so horrible they were beyond forgiveness?

I can speculate that being saturated with her grandfather's strict religion, she did feel some guilt about attempting to take the life of another human being even if it was her unwanted daughter.

If that was the case, to survive, Mother had to have been in a state of psychological denial about her murder attempts. Then she could bury any guilt she might have felt deep—deep—deep in her subconscious mind. If it was hidden, and she didn't acknowledge that part of her past, it simply didn't exist. In Montana, and then Oregon where nobody except my brother and sister knew the truth about her, she never had to answer for what she had done.

Mother had seen societies expectations for women change dramatically. If a husband shot and killed his wife, he was charged with a "passion shooting." A woman could not divorce her husband but a man could divorce his wife. He would always gain custody of any children, and the ex-wife was allowed to take only the clothes she was wearing when she left. She was twenty-five and still enslaved by her father when women won the right to vote in state and national elections.

Mother had to have had at least an inkling of the changes in women's legal status. She experienced the changes in women's role in society when she sought work with only an eighth grade education and was hired. She was an avid reader. We spent time every Saturday afternoon in the Klamath Falls library after we finished our shopping waiting for my father to finish his poker game. I read and selected an armful of books to take home and Mother read the newspapers and magazines. She expanded her world beyond her eighth grade education by reading and reading and reading. She continued that habit until she died.

Her feelings about herself and her life changed so dramatically in later years, so I don't see how she could not have had second thoughts about her abusive behavior. Mother's dishonesty kept our family secrets hidden for thirty-one years and I don't think she knew that Dean had blown the whistle on her marital status.

She apparently wasn't up to the task of acknowledging her brutality. I wonder if the taffy pulling parties we had for my neighborhood friends the last year we lived in the country were her way of saying she was sorry. It's better than nothing, but not much.

It is my strong belief that my mother went to her grave thinking she had successfully kept the questionable facts about her pregnancy, my birth, and her murder attempts secret for forty-eight years. What she didn't know is that I just didn't know how to ask the questions.

When I finally knew the truth about my suspicious birth and my mother's murder attempts, I ended the silence and broke the spell cast by years of secrecy. No more blaming the victim. No more blackmail. Only then could I begin to heal the damage caused by our family secrets. It took me a long time to forgive my mother and my first husband and it was a painful process.

To prevent relapsing back into the dysfunctional quagmire that was my life for far too long, I live by my Five Commandments. Every day I tell myself to remember what works for me:

Commandment One—Refuse to be a victim. You can be "victimized" by people but you do not have to succumb to being a victim. Work through the pain and let it go—don't relive it over and over. Rise above the circumstances and move on.

Commandment Two— Defend your personal boundaries. Wish *them* well and send *them* good thoughts, but spend as little time as possible with people who look at the world from a negative point of view, who have to put other people down to feel good about themselves, who won't accept responsibility for their actions, or who think they know what's best for you. Counter their negative energy with a statement that neutralizes their message. Disagree when someone makes demeaning comments about a person because of a perceived "difference." Silence is agreement. Refuse to give their negative energy access to your body and values even if it is a close member of your family—say a daughter-in law who refuses to apologize to a family member after blatantly misrepresenting the facts about his living standards.

Commandment Three—Do unto others as THEY would have you do unto them. I learned this interpretation of the Golden Rule from Dr. Milton Bennett, a professor at Portland State University. He pointed out that the Golden Rule: "Do unto others as *YOU* would have them do unto you" assumes that just because you like something, everyone else will like it too. You don't really know what is best for anyone except you.

Commandment Four—"If the shoe doesn't fit don't put it on." That was the good advice Mother gave me. Whatever the action or charge, if it doesn't fit say so.

Commandment Five—Do not hide anything about your past. I don't dwell on nor generally advertise the horrific parts of my life, but at times when it seems appropriate I mention my "interesting" life experiences. My message is that I wasn't Super Woman—if I could make changes to move on to a better life, anyone can. No more abuse and no more family secrets.

The tyrannical and unwritten expectations that ruled women's lives persisted well into the twentieth century. I began to get an inkling that this phenomenon existed when I was in my mid-twenties and being "different" was seen as negative. I knew I didn't fit the mold of a proper suburban woman.

Understanding that phenomenon was a start. I was a misfit in suburbia, but I wasn't afraid or ashamed of being different. Not everyone understood, and again, I didn't care.

After more years than I want to admit, I understood that my difficulty meeting the expectations of others in a suburb east of Portland called Gresham, was the fact that I grew up in the country and I had very different life experiences than my peers who had always lived in cities.

When I was still in culture shock from being a country girl in the city, I attended two diverse high school graduations that clarified why I felt like a misfit.

The first one was at Henley High School, the progressive country school I attended in southern Oregon. The Henley message was clear: No matter what the cost, protect your individuality.

The second one was in Woodburn, a small suburban town near Salem, the State capital. There, too, the message was clear: Conform. Conform. Conform. Forget about individuality. I knew immediately why I felt like a gasping fish out of water.

It was clear to me that the price for being a proper suburban woman was too high. I would never give up my individuality to conform to somebody else's standards. I would rather be a misfit.

I asked women I had grown up with in the country if they had also experienced culture shock after moving to the city and they agreed they didn't fit the norm for city women.

Girls raised in the country were expected to be assertive and do farm work just like the boys. We had to think on our feet when a steer went astray, or a cow was about to kick the milk bucket. We had to decide when to change the irrigation water and which field to direct it to. There might or might not be someone to ask for guidance. You got up early every day to feed the animals and clean their pens before getting ready for school.

Living in the country fostered assertiveness, independence, and personal responsibility. These traits were seldom seen as assets in suburbia in the 1950s. We country-women were seen as "pushy." We definitely were not the passive leave-the-decisions-to-the-men proper women.

During this era, women's identity was determined by their relationship to men and children. Depending on the circumstance, they were seen as either the wife of a man or the mother of a child: "Oh, you're Harry's wife," or "Oh, you're Tom's mother."

The perfect family was modeled after the Ozzie and Harriet television show. The house was always spotless. The kids never cried. The dinner never burned. Wives generally had little to say about the financial side of the relationship and they never had personal opinions that differed from their husbands. Television advertisements featured women waxing kitchen floors in high-heeled shoes.

I had a neighbor who actually waxed her black and white tile floors in high heels and she scolded me about a lot of things I did and didn't do. What really offended her was my nickname, Gussie. She told me more than once that "you have a perfectly good first name, Norma, and you should use it." She also spoke of her husband as "Mr. Bateman." She never used his first name in public. I respected her because she stood up for what she believed and I liked her a lot even though we were a mismatch. She was bright and could talk about things other than the kids so she had a slight streak of improper. I kept this between just us. It was our secret.

Those were the expectations that defined the proper suburban woman in the 1950s and 1960s. My neighbor fit the mold much better than I did. I wasn't even close to being the proper woman. As my mother used to say, "If the shoe doesn't fit, don't put it on."

Speaking of shoes, when I tried to buy sandals in 1951 at a Portland shoe store, the male clerk told me that my feet were too big for sandals and I shouldn't even consider wearing them because it wouldn't be "feminine." My shoe size was a 7 ½ but to the clerk in the shoe store, I was a misfit.

My friend, Jodie Sperl, made headlines in *The Oregonian* in the late 1960s when she wore a pantsuit to a Christmas party at a posh country club. A woman wearing pants was unthinkable in the 1960s.

The national discussion about women's rights that was taking place across the country had not yet reached Gresham, Oregon. My father, brother, sister, and teachers had led me to believe that I was in fact a legal "person." That was not the case in business transactions.

I was shocked to learn I couldn't get a loan for a car or anything else without a male co-signer. In the 1960s, I had to have written permission from my husband, Chet, to get my first credit card. That was beyond an insult to this country girl and it wasn't until 1974, when Congress passed the Equal Credit Opportunity Act that women were made equal to men in such matters.

I was out of step with some of my peers. I changed careers. When women I hadn't seen for some time asked what I was doing, their common response was limited to, "Oh." By the next decade, many of them had done the same things.

Divorce in suburbia in the 1960s was rare and again I was ahead of the times. A friend told me many years later that she divorced her husband because "if you could do it, I could do it, too." But not everyone agreed with her.

Mary Bergeron scolded me one day in a beauty salon as we were getting our hair cut, "It doesn't matter if Marshall beats you every day, it is your duty as a Catholic wife to take it and stay with him."

Poor Mary died of breast cancer because she didn't want to delay a trip around the world that she and her husband had planned. She told me she would wait to see about the "lump in her breast" when they returned. Unfortunately, it was a lengthy trip and the cancer killed her not too long after they returned home.

Her husband was a kind man who loved her and I suspect he would much rather have delayed the trip than her medical checkup. He wasn't given the choice. He was as much a victim as she was of the rigid expectations of the 1950s that women were inferior and there lives didn't really matter.

By the 1970s, my behavior was more mainstream. However, some men still thought I was pushy and that Chet should "control me." Or as Tex Clum told him, "That mustang needs to be haltered and broken."

It was a timing issue that didn't exist when Gresham voters elected me mayor in 1988. They expected me to get things done. I was no longer a misfit.

I can't honestly say I would have done any better than my mother if I had been enslaved for nineteen years as a non-person, a throw away daughter; or if I had been sexually abused by my mother as Marshall was for years.

To close this chapter about my hellish relationships, I had to accept the brutal fact that Mother and Marshall were abusers. Again, Ala-Non Twelve Step meetings helped me understand the key points of recovery from a life of abuse: 1. Acknowledge that the abuse happened. 2. To define myself as a victim of abuse gave my abusers absolute power over me. 3. Recovery would come from letting go and moving on without blame or denial. Going through this process has made me realize how very important it is to discuss any actions that hurt another person sooner rather than later and make amends.

But their early life experiences don't relieve them of accepting responsibility for their actions. While it is certainly true that we all do the best we can with the knowledge we have at the time, it rings hollow if the opportunity for healing and change is dismissed as unimportant.

I not only moved beyond the hurt, insecurity, and anger caused by their murderous actions, but ultimately, I thrived. I can understand and forgive my Mother with respect and love. I can understand and forgive Marshall with respect because he, too, was violated by the one person in the world he should have been able to trust—his mother.

Marshall needs to acknowledge that he was an abuser and stop blaming me for his actions. Awake or asleep, he was the monster in my nightmare life. He needs to admit that he tried to kill me four times—twice by neglect and twice purposely:

1. I would have bled to death waiting for the ambulance he called instead of taking me to the hospital immediately when I hemorrhaged after childbirth. As a physician, he knew that it would

take at least twenty minutes for an ambulance to get to Gresham. I had to lie in my own blood that covered half of our bathroom floor until Dr. Langley rescued me. During our divorce hearing, Marshall admitted to Judge Carl Dahl that he had refused to help me other than calling for an ambulance.

2. If I hadn't regained consciousness after I fainted in the bathroom and was then able to crawl some thirty feet on my hands and knees to the telephone to call Dr. Catlow and an ambulance, I would have died from the staph infection raging though by body. Marshall refused to help me and admitted this gruesome fact to Judge Dahl at our divorce hearing.

3. He terrorized me for years and then gave me enough barbiturates to commit suicide.

4. If I hadn't thrown my car keys at Marshall and distracted him so I escape he would have either beaten or choked me to death. The infrared photos ordered by Dr. Fisher were vivid proof of Marshall's intentions. Marshall needs to make amends for his abusive actions and admit that I did have a right to divorce him.

A personal value that has helped me understand and accept my past is my belief in a Higher Power. Since I was five years old, laying in the grass high in the Rocky Mountains, looking up at the blue sky and the clouds, I have felt certain there is a Higher Power. IT was a feeling of security that was both real and unreal. IT was something somewhere. I didn't have a name for IT but I knew I could ask for guidance and protection, and I have done so several times a day since that first discovery.

It wasn't something I learned from my mother since she never set foot in a church after she was freed from her DeVoss slave masters. It wasn't something I learned in church since I was in a church only one time in my first eighteen years. Our neighbors asked Mother if they could take me to their church, and as usual without talking to me about it, she just sent me off with our good Christian neighbors who had just sold us sacks of grain mixed with dock weed seed. I have no idea what denomination the church was but I remember the wild singing and loud yelling scared me enough that I went into my usual escape response: I sneaked out the door and walked home. It was not a short walk.

I have not had much success in being a church member. The Catholics would have me believe that I should kneel on the floor every night so my husband could give me a blessing. This was the same man who tried to kill me four times.

A Unity minister criticized me because I wasn't able to "heal" my worn out knee and had surgery. He was also advising diabetics to stop taking their insulin.

My good friend, Betty Schedeen, convinced me to try her Episcopalian Church. There are two in Gresham and she loved them both. Betty was a woman who always had a pocket full of Crosses' and gave them to anyone and everyone. An example: Betty never left a restaurant without giving every person a silver cross and a word or two about Jesus Christ.

My problem with that particular church was the strong perfume worn by many of the women attending the services. It wasn't that I had a screw loose, which I am certain some of the church goers thought. According to a representative from the U.S. Environmental Protection Agency, who I heard on National Public Radio, perfume lovers have a halo of ozone and formaldehyde surrounding them as it decomposes.

That explained why the perfume-filled church made my chemical sensitivities rage and my immune system cringe. The priest told me to just sit in the back of the tiny, tiny church. He obviously didn't think it was important, so he didn't ask these women to give up perfume for an hour on Sunday morning.

So I tried the other one of Betty's preferred churches and it was perfume-free. But when my second and forever husband was dying, the priest said he didn't offer prayers for him from the altar because of "privacy" concerns. Yet he wouldn't correct a total lie printed in the church newsletter. The "Church Mouse" had written that my son and daughter in-law from Idaho were moving to Gresham to take care of me the year it seemed I was dying. The head lay person of the church, with the title of Warden, agreed to let the Church Mouse's inaccuracy stand. A church that was not concerned about truthfulness in one of its official documents was not one that I wanted to support.

I didn't have the courage to try another church. So I went back to the church that had never let me down, my own church high in the Montana Rocky Mountains with a carpet of green grass, mountainous crater walls, and an endless ceiling of blue sky and puffy white clouds. Every day, several times a day, I ask for guidance from my Higher Power: I close my eyes and take myself to that safe and beautiful mountain hideaway.

I didn't ever plan my life except to get an education, and I swear I never set goals to check off after I accomplished something because I don't worry about my future. I have found that the Universe provides opportunities that I wouldn't even have thought possible. Thank you, God! I don't have to bless Mother and Marshall, but for my own well-being I have to forgive them with great sincerity. I deserve serenity.

CHAPTER EIGHT

THE LOVE OF MY LIFE

L ike my brother and sister, some excellent schoolteachers, and several outstanding physicians, Chet McRobert also helped save my life.

I first met Chet when Marshall and I bought a new car from McRobert Motor Company, the Gresham Ford franchise purchased with Mr. Carr in 1930 by his father, Chester.

We got to know Chet and his wife, Delores, through dinner and bridge groups. In a town of three thousand people, our paths crossed frequently. One day in 1960, I spotted Chet in his Thunderbird convertible, with the top down, stopped at a traffic light in the opposite lane from me, at the intersection of Sandy Boulevard and Broadway Avenue in Portland. He motioned toward the Poor Richard's Pub & Restaurant located across the street. I was early for a gynecologist appointment so I thought, "Why not?" We had coffee and conversation and went our separate ways without either of us mentioning the possibility of a repeat performance. Chet was happy in his marriage. I was persevering in mine.

Several weeks later, Chet was waiting for me in front of the Portland YWCA building where I was scheduled for swimming lessons with friends. I wondered how he knew I would be there but as usual with my head in the sand approach to life, I didn't ask. Later I learned the "baby sitter" told him I was taking swimming lessons, and in those days that meant I would be at the Portland YWCA.

He had a message that would change both our lives forever: His wife, Delores, was dead. She was pregnant and her obstetrician had prescribed Dexedrine for energy in the daytime and Seconal for sleep at night. She added alcohol to her doctor's mix of uppers and downers and died sitting in a chair in their living room.

There was no understanding then of how alcohol increased the sedative affect of barbiturates. She had unknowingly mixed herself a deadly concoction robbing herself of a third chance to have a healthy baby girl that both she and Chet were happily awaiting. They were still grieving over losing two other baby girls who died shortly after their premature births and they had high hopes for this third attempt to add a daughter to their family.

Chet needed somebody to talk to. He loved Dee and he missed her terribly. He wondered what he could have done differently to prevent her death. He felt guilty that he hadn't awakened in the night and realized that she wasn't in bed. He wondered how he would be able to raise their two sons, Marc and Brad, without her. He mourned losing yet another baby girl. It was almost more than he could endure and I was a safe shoulder for him to cry on.

We talked on the phone. We talked in Washington Park. We talked at Poor Richard's Pub & Restaurant. We talked at his house. Later, we talked at my house. With my lifelong experience of having male friends with no sexual innuendoes or expectations, it didn't seem unusual to me. I didn't live in a neighborhood with another girl until I was thirteen.

Due to the conspiracy of silence between women about their abusive relationships, and having fled from the patriarchal church in dismay, I also needed a friend to talk with about my problems and I was not interested in complicating our friendship with sex. My feeling about sex at that point in my life was it was much more trouble than it was worth.

Chet knew my male trust level registered a frigid minus-zero. My "Montana Distrust Signal," nurtured through high school was once again alive and well and screaming warnings not to get too close to any man. It was a danger zone.

I continued my destructive relationship with Marshall Brown misguidedly thinking that having another child would help. Chet didn't question my misguided thinking or the medical treatment I was getting to be able to have a baby. He seemed pleased when I told him the treatments were successful.

If I hadn't become desperately ill and pushed to the breaking point, I think our relationship as confidants would have eventually ended. Chet was dating several women and thinking about his future. I wanted him to have the happiness he so deserved.

I didn't notice any Third Eye warnings, "He isn't what you think he is" when I was around Chet. He didn't put on airs. He was what he was. He didn't tell me what to do and how and when to do it. He didn't make demands of me. There didn't seem to be any hidden expectations. He was gentle but strong and like my brother and sister he seemed to care about me as a human being.

Was it too good to be true? I tested him when I was in the hospital just before Tim was born. I showed him my four-foot long incision and the protruding catheter that so offended Marshall's sensitivity. Chet touched it lightly and his only concern was that it might cause me pain. He won my heart then and there. Chet's message of encouragement gave me hope and the strength to live.

Our trust and respect for each other gradually grew into love. One of the best things about being with Chet was that I didn't have to pay for good times with abuse and pain. It was a two-way relationship of give and take and I felt safe.

With Chet's caring love and patience, over time my "stay away from me" defense wall gradually weakened and collapsed, piece-by-piece. My divorce attorney, Carlton Reiter, knew about my friendship with Chet. He counseled me that unless I was very sure that I wanted to marry Chet, I should not meet with him even to talk until the divorce was final. I wasn't sure I wanted to be married ever again to anyone, even Chet. I didn't completely trust what I was feeling for him so I heeded Mr. Reiter's warning.

In a total lapse of intelligence and confidence, I let Marshall talk me into reconciliation. I told Chet that I had to give my marriage one more chance. He didn't try to talk me out of it but when Marshall and I left for a weekend in San Francisco, Chet attempted suicide. We never talked about it which is hard to believe now but we were both wounded sparrows and I suspect denial was easier for both of us. Most likely, I didn't want to feel responsible.

During our attempt at reconciliation, Marshall was back to being abusive, "You're too stupid to do anything but take care of the house and kids" routine. After a couple of weeks, I realized just how really stupid I had been and called Mr. Reiter to reopen the divorce application. He had put it on hold instead of taking it off the docket. He knew the reconciliation wasn't going to miraculously change Marshall. The divorce proceeded on schedule—and before no-fault divorce in Oregon, that meant slowly, very slowly.

It was cumbersome as well as slow. Mr. Reiter instructed me to keep a written record of everyone I met and talked with and any witnesses that could corroborate my presence for every fifteen-minute period of every day and night during the year and a half preceding the divorce hearing. Chet's name was not on the list.

We talked by phone about his sons, his personal life, since he was dating women, and about my life that included only my three sons, and a full class-load at the University of Portland, which Marshall had tried to sabotage.

Marshall called me at 2 AM on the very morning I was scheduled to take the SAT college entry exams and said, "You're too stupid. You won't pass." I slammed down the phone, went back to sleep, and passed the SAT with flying colors. Success is the best revenge. I also asked my sons to talk with their father only about their activities.

My divorce was final on February 6, 1964. I was free of Marshall Brown FOREVER. On February 26th, Chet took me out to dinner at the Rose Room to celebrate my birthday. We began to officially date as a romantic couple. It was scary at first, but as our trust in each other grew more secure, we set a wedding date. The limited options I had in my first marriage because I lacked a profession still haunted me. I was determined to get my nursing degree from Clark College as planned. Chet supported my educational goals, and he understood my need for financial independence, and that finishing nursing school was a high priority. My second marriage was as good as the first one was bad.

We were married at Chet's Wallula house on August 15, 1965 by our friend, and Justice of the Peace, Sidney Bartels with just a few of our closest friends attending. We don't have a wedding picture of just the two of us. It was a marriage of seven people: Chet and me, Marc, Skip, Bradley, Gregory, and Timothy; two cats: Snowball and Tiger; and one dog: a Basset Hound named Flash. It was a challenge. That's life.

A challenge could also describe our honeymoon. Chet won a trip to Portugal for exceeding Ford Motor Company sales quotas and he made the reservations before we were married so we weren't officially listed as husband and wife en route from New York. A prominent Portland dealer's wife thought it was scandalous that Ford had allowed an unmarried couple to go on the trip. Most people knew the real story but Chet delighted in keeping her in the dark about our marriage.

After a night in New York City, and an uneventful flight across the Atlantic Ocean, we really enjoyed the breath taking beauty of Portugal. We watched with fascination day after day as workers on the beach in front of our Estoril de Sol hotel built a sand brick wall, which would then be washed away by the incoming high tide forcing them to start all over again the next day building a new sand brick wall. We agreed there was a life lesson to be learned in that experience. From that time until Chet's last days, we had a secret code to explain if our day had gone poorly. If it was an "Estoril de Sol" day, we knew it hadn't been the best of days. That, too, is life.

We looked forward to the Atlantic cruise back to New York City. It went well until an uninvited guest joined us: a hurricane that lasted three days. The waves were higher than the ship. The drop to the bottom of the trough wasn't as terrifying as the climb up the other side when it felt as though you were being catapulted right off the ship. Chet was one of only three people on the ship besides the crew who didn't get seasick. The rest of us were strapped to our beds and very heavily sedated with Compazine to keep us asleep, safe, ad out of the way. We added a "Hurricane Day" to our classification of what kind of day we had and it was one point higher than an "Estoril de Sol" day.

The condition of our cruise ship, the *Mauritania* was a major concern to Chet and several other car dealers who were also airplane pilots and knew something about mechanics. They were sure they felt the ship shudder at a certain point in the rotation of the engine's screw propeller. Just before our cruise,

Cunard Cruise Line officials had announced that our Portugal trip was the *Mauritania's* last voyage. We hoped we wouldn't go down with her to the graveyard for old, worn-out ships. Ford Motor Company must have gotten a real deal on that reward trip. What a reward! Chet and I didn't go on another cruise for thirty-six years. We finally braved a cruise to Alaska where we could see land at all times.

You could say that our honeymoon got us off to such a rough start that everything afterward seemed easy. Sometimes it was easy. Other times it wasn't easy. Back home we settled in with two families. My sons and I moved into Chet's house. Later on, we realized we should have started our life together in a house that was new to everyone with no ownership or territorial rights issues for those who were there first. That was a small hurdle we had to get over and then it was back to reality. I had to concentrate on school.

My relationship with Chet was all about healing and communication and helped me move past the wounds from my abuse and family secrets. We were ahead of our time in creating a blended family and there was little information on how to go about making it work. It wasn't easy. With limited professional help and a commitment to honesty and openness we learned from each other. It wouldn't have worked if Chet and I hadn't trusted and loved each other enough to form a solid parental team: a team that the boys couldn't weaken, coercing one of us to take sides against the other to get their way on whatever was the problem of the day.

Chet understood what it meant to run a household. His five years of being a single father made him a very understanding husband and he insisted that we have full-time help so I could take a full load of classes. Ada Witt was a great help to me when I went back to school full time as a thirty-two year old single mother and college freshman. Ada agreed to take on all five boys. We couldn't have done it without her. Ada then started attending Gresham Senior Center meetings, met a man who became her husband and decided to retire. We missed her, but wished her well. Florece Harper, amiable and very, very capable then helped us until she had to quit for health reasons.

So I put a "household help wanted" ad in *The Gresham Outlook*'s classified section. The same day the weekly newspaper was delivered, a man came to our door, inquiring about the ad. "I hope you won't hold it against me because I'm a man," he said. He got my full attention. Although I had been very publicly opposed to gender discrimination, I had to admit that was thinking, "I will still be in my bathrobe."

I also had to admit that it was more than a little hypocritical for me to consider not hiring someone just because he was a man. We talked, the references for his janitorial company were solid, and I hired Michael Elia. Mike took wonderful care of us for twenty years and then he had the nerve to retire to Arizona. We wished him well, and hoped the lucky people in Arizona understood what a good man they were getting.

Chet and I faced territorial problems. How could his sons, Marc and Brad, not feel invaded when they had previously had a father and house all to themselves for five years and then four people, a Basset Hound, and an orange tabby cat moved in? Teamwork and the tincture of time resolved the *"whose house is it"* issue.

We supported each other in whatever activity we were involved in as well as our sons' school activities. We enjoyed golf and skiing as a family, and we attended our son's band concerts, baseball games, swim meets, golf tournaments, and go-cart and ski races. We swam in our pool winter and summer and the guys could invite their friends to join them. It was also an unobtrusive way to know where they were and what they were doing.

Our pool and three others nearby attracted a following of Mallard ducks. They ate the corn we put out for them, and the ones that adopted us—and I swear I'm telling the truth, the whole truth, and nothing but the truth— never, ever pooped in the pool. I tried to chase a female mallard out of the pool by spraying water on her so I could swim duck-free. She just raised one wing at a time saying, "a little more on the right side, please." I gave up and joined her.

I skipped car-racing events at Portland International Raceway. That was a "guy" thing that Chet and the boys looked forward to every year. However, when Chet sponsored a racecar, and it was personal, I ventured out to the track. I really enjoyed watching our guy's go-cart races. Chet built the go-carts and the guys looked forward to putting the 'pedal to the metal' at a community racetrack not far away in Damascus. It was less about racing to win and more about just having fun. Marge even took the wheel and made several laps on her visits north.

Although I was a student getting up at 3:00 AM to study before going to the hospital, I saw to that we had a more than adequate breakfast every morning. No more Coke and chocolate cake for breakfast. We also had a sit down dinner every night. We had a hand bell that rang loud enough to wake the dead. Our neighbors knew exactly when the McRobert family had dinner.

Brad was responsible for the family laundry detail. He had driven away several housekeepers after his mother died and he was determined to drive me away as well. He said to me in his best Master to Servant, I am the General in charge of this Department tone of voice, "Where are my clean socks?" By the end of that day the guys each had a laundry bag and had received a lesson in how to use the washer. Five-year old Tim, who changed shirts several times a day, reached down to his bedroom floor where he discarded the used ones, picked up his green football shirt and said, "I can wear this again." They got it.

Brad said many years later, when his friends were getting married when they were barely out of high school, "I don't have to get married to have somebody to wash my socks or cook." Learning to cook wasn't that difficult. Cooking is like a chemistry lab experiment. If you can read, you can turn out a reasonable product.

There was a household chore chart that rotated jobs between the guys: emptying dishwasher, etc. They could help Chet with shop projects and learn to use power tools and how to repair whatever fell apart.

Chet, being used to people signing in an out in a business setting, designed and built a Family Check In and Check Out blackboard with a list of geographical areas that were assigned a number— Area One, Area Two, etc. When we were out and about we selected the appropriate Area Number and hung it next to our names. Chet being a pilot devoted a section on the blackboard's right side for our "Expected Time of Arrival" home. It helped us track each other and wasn't invasive or over protective.

To counter the "always on the run" syndrome that families in suburbia are famous for we had various spots outside in our yard where we could escape and enjoy a quiet garden setting and listen for a breeze in the trees or the water running in the creek in our entry way. There is nothing quite like floating on an air mattress in your very private swimming pool to get off the treadmill of life. That was before Google Earth satellites provided anyone and everyone access to all our back yards and what we were and weren't wearing that particular day.

The guys had privacy if they wanted it in their own private bedroom, and company if they didn't. They could read a book, listen to music, or go outside and look up at our century old elm tree and listen to the birds sing, watch the antics of our many squirrels, and enjoy the summer breeze.

For a short time we had a rope tied to the ancient elm tree that they loved to swing on. We took it down, however, after I counted seventeen kids in our back yard waiting for turns on the rope and not one of them was ours. People we didn't even know were dropping their kids off in the culdesac that bordered our back yard to swing on the apparently infamous rope.

Chet gave special attention to the boys. He coached their Little League teams, helped with projects for school and Cub Scouts and Boy Scouts, showed them how to use his shop tools, and saw that they got to early practice of whatever sport they were in at school.

The three sons I brought to our new family lost touch with their father over time. It was caused by his inconsistency. For example, he cancelled a visitation with them just before Christmas because he "had to perform surgery." As we drove past his office some thirty minutes later on the way to the Rexall Drug Store, we noticed his office parking lot was full of cars that the boys recognized as belonging to their father's friends. He was having an office Christmas party. As Tim said, "He lied to us."

Marshall took me to Court about child support. He claimed I was squandering it because Chet would not accept the money for the boys living expenses. I had invested every cent of it in Boeing, Georgia Pacific, 3M, and Ford Motor Company in separate accounts under their individual names. The judge scolded me for not asking to have the amount of child support increased. Visitations were contentious and that too was a legal issue. Marshall brought it on himself. The boys no longer wanted him as a father. They thought of Chet as their father.

This led to a discussion of adoption. We made it a family affair. I adopted Brad and Marc. Chet adopted Skip and Tim. Greg felt he would be disloyal to the father who adopted him first so we agreed it was best that he not be adopted a second time. It was always interesting watching people try to figure out which boys belonged to which parent. They were wrong most of the time.

Although Chet's mother and father's relationship was more traditional than ours, they were wonderful to me and accepted my sons as their grandchildren. They had not always had an easy life. Father and son shared the name, Chester Arthur. I am going to speak of Chester Senior as Chester and Chester Junior as Chet.

Because Chester married a Roman Catholic, Evelyn Adler, he was disowned and shunned by his family. I didn't ask and Chet never mentioned whether his grandparents, William and Rhoda McRobert practiced a particular religion that mandated the shunning. Chester never wavered from his choice. He married the woman he loved instead of someone approved by his father.

Of Chester's twelve siblings only one brother, Eldon, kept in contact with him. McRobert is a common name in Washington County west of Portland because many descendants of William and Rhoda live there. We don't know any of them.

The story we were told about Chester's family was that his father, William, as a teenager came to the Oregon country with other pioneers traveling in a wagon train on the Oregon Trail; and there were tales about being a stagecoach driver and chased by Indians, and that he drove across the Columbia River when it was frozen solid with several feet of ice. He was tough.

He had to be tough to survive the dangers of the Oregon Trail and the pioneer life he had chosen. His relationship with wife, Rhoda, and their thirteen children was no different than other families in America: Women and children were the property of their husband and father. William issued edicts and everyone obeyed except Chester and his brother, Eldon.

I wanted to confirm the shunning and the Oregon Trail stories, and couldn't find a William McRobert in any of the Oregon Trail web sites, so I called Directory Assistance for Eldon McRobert. I found Chester's brother's eighty-seven year old grandson living in Hillsboro in Washington County with his wife of sixty-seven years, Theresa. He didn't hang up when I told him who I was and why I was calling.

Eldon confirmed the shunning edict and the Oregon Trail history and added that his great grandfather, William, was from Wisconsin, and had married Rhoda Parsons. So our stories matched.

William is probably spinning in his grave with the thought of Chester's daughter in-law and his great grandson not honoring the proud patriarch's shunning edict. I hope William with more than a century to think about his actions, welcomed Evelyn, Chester, and Chet to the other side and made amends. It may be too much to ask that he will also welcome me when my turn on this planet ends.

Although William died in 1930, the year Chet was born, he was almost a teenager before his father began Christmas visits to Gayles Creek so he could get to know his grandmother.

Knowing full well that William despised her because she was a Roman Catholic, Evelyn showed amazing compassion when it came to her father in-law. Compassion that makes me makes me wonder at her kindness when I water the McRobert Meadow Rue plant on my deck.

The story is that William gave Rhoda a Meadow Rue plant dug from the Gayles Creek woods near their home as a wedding gift. The Meadow Rue is a subspecies of the Buttercup family only taller with small round leaves in groups of three, growing to two or three feet tall. Rhoda gave a start from the Gayles Creek Meadow Rue plant to Chester, and Evelyn saw to it that I received a start to keep the tradition going. I've seen to it that Rhoda's great grandsons also have a

Meadow Rue so they can have at least one good thought about their great grandfather.

In a family of thirteen children, none of them could have received much individual attention from their parents and Chester brought that hands-off parenting model to his family after he married Evelyn.

After Chester died I got to know Evelyn on a more personal level. She told me that her parents left the children alone for months at a time every winter while they visited relatives in Wisconsin. Evelyn was the second oldest in a family of four. The two older girls took care of the family until their parents returned in the spring. They managed to keep up with their schoolwork and nobody from the Forest Grove schools or community stepped in to help or take over the family. The annual disappearing act with children forced to become surrogate parents was treated as normal by the real parents and there was never any discussion or explanation for the long absences.

Family friends have said that Chet was not given the support they thought he should have had from either of his parents. For example, Chet's breakfast was just a Coca Cola and a big piece of chocolate cake that he grabbed as he left for school.

Chocolate cake and Coca Cola for breakfast must not have seemed like neglect to a father who was one of thirteen children, and to a mother who had to fend not only for herself, but also for her siblings every winter.

Chet couldn't count on emotional support from his parents. They saw that he had roof over his head, a limited choice of food, clothes to wear, and a car to drive. When he drove a tractor through a plate glass window at the dealership at a young age he was responsible for getting himself a block away to Dr. Hughes office to get his knee sewn back together. The good doctor continued his parent's lack of concern. He didn't give Chet anything to deaden the pain. For the rest of his life, Chet had to be lying flat to get any kind of medical treatment because he would faint and fall out of the chair at the sight of a needle or a medical instrument.

Although they never mentioned it to either Chet or me, I suspect they didn't approve of my choice to continue going to school after we married. Some of his friends objected to my going to school and one told him to, "Just say no!" Another asked, "Can't you control her?" His answer was, "Why would I want to?"

That was the first time, but not the last time that my departure from the behavioral norm for women would be an issue for others. It was never an issue for Chet. He took some heat about the state of his manhood from some men who were not quite as secure and enlightened as he was. He loved me and I loved him. That's all that mattered. We didn't care what people thought about our relationship. That doesn't mean we didn't have some major issues to resolve.

Chet's parents unintentionally taught him that emotional uncertainty was the norm for families. This became apparent two years after we married when Skip, Greg, and Tim were with their father for a week and I came home to an empty house—no Chet, no Marc, no Brad, and no message where they were. His parents didn't know where they were. They reappeared several days later and said they had flown to Jackson Hole, Wyoming "for some time alone."

I made it clear that not telling me they were leaving was a deal killer. I didn't want to be married to a man that treated me so uncaringly and I informed him that I had filed for divorce. As Chet left he said, "The way to raise children is to keep them guessing where they stand."

I didn't understand then, but the William McRobert legacy was playing out in my life. I asked myself how the man who seemed so caring and gentle could end up being a jerk, a different kind of jerk, but still a Jerk with a capital J. And why hadn't I picked up on that particular psychological flaw? The difference the second time around, however, was that I wasn't willing to put up with it for even one minute. However, what's good for the gander is also good for the goose so I took my three sons to San Francisco for a week on Chet's dime.

After a month of seeing that I was not going to back down, Chet agreed to see a counselor and after I was certain he was in fact doing so he moved back into the Wallula house. In that time, Chet had come to the conclusion that he didn't want a relationship similar to his parents and was willing to do whatever it took to undue the patterns he had learned from them.

Chet kept his promise. We worked to understand ourselves, and each other, and moved on to another thirty-five years of marriage. Chet was once again the man I had previously known as trustworthy and the man I had given myself permission to love. It wasn't easy but we were dedicated to making our marriage relationship a positive experience for each of us and for our children. We acknowledged, "that it would take time and that real change wouldn't happen over night." But we wanted to learn how to make our relationship work.

Over time, Chet made me feel loved without feeling stifled or controlled. Because he had lost one wife suddenly, he was afraid something might happen to me. He was nervous about me driving to Mt. Hood Meadows to go skiing with friends. I assured him that "growing up in southern Oregon, I had many years of experience driving in the snow." He countered with "the water content of the wet Mount Hood snow is higher and more slippery to drive on than the dry powder snow you're used to." So I suggested a trial run to the mountain with him as a passenger. I passed his competency test and he stopped worrying.

Chet took care of me and that was something entirely new to me. He tracked the mileage on my car and when it was time for oil changes and tune-ups, he would say, "I'll trade cars with you today." He did that for thirty-seven years, until his health deteriorated and then he tried to teach me about cars and their maintenance needs.

I can check the air pressure and use Chet's air compressor to fill the tires when necessary. That's the full extent of me doing anything to cars and I hate having to change windshield wipers. Gas stations were Service stations with a capital S when I was responsible for my own car. I didn't have to know anything about cars except to fill the gas tank and get the oil changed. I get my Escape to the dealership on time for whatever it needs.

I'm still one of those 1950s women when it comes to talking about sex. I will say, however, that there was always a small suitcase in the trunk of Chet's T-Bird packed for an overnight sleepover at a hotel if we were so inclined after a night out on the town. Our babysitters understood and willingly extended their shifts. I have recommended the "packed bag in the trunk" routine to several friends.

Many years after we married, I noticed a circle with numbers on some of the days in Chet's appointment calendar. I asked him about the numbers and his answer was interesting. I can only say that it is a very fortunate woman who marries a man who is more interested in his partner's pleasure than his own.

Overcoming the trials and tribulations we faced over the years created such a strong emotional bond of love and trust between us that we were two souls joined as one. The mechanics of sex seemed secondary.

Taking time for ourselves was wonderful on an impromptu basis but thinking long-term, we knew we needed to do something to help keep our partnership strong. We didn't want to end up as strangers from the demands of a busy family. There were far too many examples of couples that had devoted their lives to their children's activities, and when the children left home and they had nobody to talk to except each other found they were strangers. Divorce was the common solution.

We wanted to continue to be lovers and best friends as we grew old together. So we promised ourselves time away from the daily duties of our life and scheduled ahead of time on a regular basis. We enjoyed our monthly weekend "getaways" as we called them. It didn't have to be an exotic or expensive trip. Often it was a weekend at the Portland Hilton Hotel or time to put our feet up and watch the boats go by on the Columbia River at the Red Lion at Jantzen Beach or walk the beaches on the Oregon coast or enjoy the mountains at a resort near Mount Hood. The venue was only important as a place to give us private time together with no kids and no phones ringing. We did get some strange looks though registering for a weekend stay when we lived only thirty minutes away.

We scheduled longer trips every three months. One of the most memorable was our 35th anniversary trip to Bora Bor. We signed up for a boat trip around the island. Until our boatman slowed the boat and revved the motor several times, I thought to myself, "ho hum, it was the usual circle the island boat trip." But the manta rays recognized the boatman's approach signal and as soon as he anchored the boat, the manta rays swam toward it. The water was quite shallow so you could stand in the water and see them up close and personal, but I wanted to see what they would do if I swam toward them. And then a miracle happened. A manta ray slid underneath me and then cradled me in its uplifted wings. It lasted only a few seconds, but I will remember it always as one of the most special moments of my life. It was definitely not the usual ho hum circle the island boat trip.

There wasn't anything Chet and I couldn't share with each other. He held me in his arms while I sobbed for what seemed like hours after my brother saw to it that

I knew about my birth status. He reassured me that the new information didn't change his love for me. He held me in his arms while I sobbed after my sister told me about my mother's attempts to kill me—the unwanted daughter. Chet's loving acceptance made me love him even more.

Chet also held me in his arms while I cried after attending a conference at Portland State University and heard Betty Freidan speak about her book THE FEMININE MYSTIQUE. Her message about expanding women's lives somehow opened old wounds inflicted by my mother, my first husband, and the Klamath County Elks Club—a slight on my gender that I have never forgotten.

In the middle of the night, in a fit of rage, I burned the Elks Lodge Scholarship Committee letter that said they were giving the four-year college scholarship not to me, the highest-ranking candidate, but to a boy with the second-highest score. I would give anything to have that letter now. I'd frame it and put it on the wall with my various and sundry awards.

Chet understood my need for independence, and most importantly, he understood that having an independent wife didn't make him less of a man. Chet knew I loved him absolutely and unconditionally. I knew Chet loved me absolutely and unconditionally. We didn't have to be in the same room to communicate our love for each other.

Chet supported my desire to leave nursing. He applauded at graduation ceremonies when I received my Bachelor's and Master's degrees. He raved about my news reports. He even approved of my going into politics and campaigned with me door to door for months before my successful election as mayor. He never felt threatened by my success and I wasn't threatened by his success. Owning and managing an auto dealership, being active in civic organizations, and having many interests outside work, Chet was strong and successful in his own right. I never begrudged Chet's time spent away from home and he never complained about my busy schedule. We treasured out time together.

The McRobert's and the White's owned AeroCredit, a company that financed and insured small general aviation aircraft. The Beechcraft Bonanza was a company plane but by the 1960s, Chet was the one who did most of the flying and was responsible for maintenance. Lunch in Seattle or San Francisco still left time for business in Gresham. Summer family vacations in Sun Valley required a bigger plane but the Bonanza met most of our needs. None of the boys seemed concerned about flying in a single engine airplane with one pilot. It was me, the Grinch, who worried what I would do if Chet had a heart attack and I had to be talked down by the air traffic controllers in the tower like the terrified women in the movies.

I wanted to be able to land the plane if necessary. But you can't learn to land without learning how to take off and fly the airplane without killing yourself or someone else. There is the instrument panel, turning and banking, direction of the wind and its affect on take-off and landing procedures, traffic patterns, slow flight, what to do in a stall, and a daunting list of other things to know. So I took flying lessons from a FLIGHTCRAFT instructor, Doug Black, at Portland International Airport (PDX) with Chet's blessing.

Doug agreed with my assessment that I was ready to fly solo after a month of almost daily lessons. My first solo flight was from PDX to the Scappoose Airport in the days when small airplanes could safely fly out of an international airport. We had flown the route during a couple of lessons and all I had to do was follow the Columbia River to Scappoose about twenty miles west of PDX.

Doug instructed me to get out of the plane after landing in Scappoose and pick a long piece of dry grass by the runway. When I arrived back at PDX, I was to get out of the plane with the grass sticking out of the side of my mouth as proof that I had actually made it to Scappoose. I followed his directions implicitly. It was great fun!

I flew three more solo flights but when the fall rains began I was grounded. I was busy with other things and never flew cross-country. I achieved what I set out to do though and flew the "right" seat with Chet thereafter knowing that if I had to be talked down to make an emergency landing, I wouldn't make it worse by being terrified. I wasn't yet flying in my dreams and while that is more exciting than flying airplanes, I am grateful for the opportunity of learning to fly.

In 1994, Chet had a minor stroke followed by nine years of fainting spells and increasing muscular weakness. After he attended a meeting in Prague, Czechoslovakia our physician, Douglas Grossnickle, M.D., said he had a name for something he had noticed in a few patients over time but couldn't interest neurologists in researching: Sub-Cortical Ischemic Brain Syndrome, or very small hemorrhages in the brain cells that affected motor function by weakening the muscles. He said it had been thoroughly researched in Europe for years, but there was little that could be done to slow its advance.

As he got weaker, Chet worried that he couldn't "rescue" me if I had trouble on the road so I always called him when I was in between meetings or running errands. It was always good to hear his voice and know that he, too, was OK. No matter where I was, or who it was I was meeting with, my cell phone was always turned on. I said, "I want Chet to be able to reach me any where at any time." The only people who gave me strange looks were those who didn't always want others to know of their whereabouts.

After I gave our financial adviser an unequivocal No to his question in November 2002 about whether we had considered moving into a condominium,

Chet brought it up the following January. Looking back, I think he wanted me settled before he died. When I had our swimming pool filled with dirt and planted a rose garden, he knew my heart was not into keeping up a house and yard that was much bigger than what we needed.

So we moved into what I once called "the ugly little brown houses" on the first fairway of the Persimmon Country Club three miles south of our Wallula house. I no longer think of the little brown Golf Villas as ugly, and I don't have to worry about yard upkeep or putting money aside for a new roof, etc. Chet said it was like being on vacation with the tree-covered buttes and protected wildlife corridors surrounded by green everywhere. He enjoyed seeing an occasional deer making its way south on the fairway to turn south and continue its travel. The occasional raccoon and coyote sighting is great fun. I especially enjoy listening to the coyotes bay at the moon. Coyotes are another "back to my roots" amenity because I loved hearing the coyotes howl in the moon light on Miller Hill when I lived in southern Oregon. Coyote serenades sooth my soul. It is peaceful here in the "ugly little brown houses."

As news about Chet's worsening health situation spread through the community, former employees called wanting to talk to him before he died. Chet valued the employees at McRobert Motor Company. He wasn't just spouting platitudes. His beliefs were based on the principle that employees were real people and very important. The dealership staff responded with loyalty, hard work, and friendship. I understood their feelings because that's how he treated me. I was his wife and a person of value.

I don't think Chet realized the impact he had on the people who worked at the dealership. They came to our home to tell Chet he had helped them personally as well as professionally. Their collective message was that he was more than an employer to them and that his quiet counseling had helped them resolve personal issues and even save marriages. The outpouring of gratitude was the most amazing and wonderful phenomenon and it meant a great deal to Chet.

Until the last three days of his life, Chet's mind was sharp. Talking was difficult for him but we had forty years of conversations to remember. He was up and about with the help of a three-wheeled walker (his go-cart, as we called it) and he could dress and feed himself. For someone who had been active in civic affairs, was an accomplished pilot and athlete, and had managed a successful business, physical restrictions must have been difficult. But he never complained.

Chet was especially disappointed that he could not fulfill his dream of being a volunteer to help in disaster recovery efforts. He was a volunteer in the Service Corps of Retired Executives (SCORE), a subsidiary of the federal Small Business Administration (SBA) for ten years, advising owners of new businesses. Since he knew the ins and outs of the SBA, he wanted to help businesses recover after hurricanes or floods or whatever the disaster might be. It was to be a team effort with my political background having worked with the Federal Emergency Management Agency (FEMA) and my work with the media. But it was not to be.

Through conference calls with our physician, I made certain that Chet knew what the increasing muscle weakness meant as the number of tiny hemorrhages increased and destroyed the part of his brain that controlled muscle strength and movement. He refused to accept that death was near and continued his exercises, in hope of getting stronger.

As his esophagus and stomach muscles weakened and he couldn't swallow, I knew that the aspiration pneumonia that was to be Chet's death sentence was near. I scheduled our Thanksgiving and Christmas family festivities in late October, but I forgot to have Chet open his Christmas presents. The bronze cat that I knew would make him smile sits in a place of honor on the fireplace mantle. Every time I see that cat, I smile and think of Chet.

Our cat, Tiger Two stayed by Chet's side. They were best buddies. Tiger developed a cancerous tumor in his mouth and was facing death along with his human buddy. Chet was adamant, and so was I, that we ignore the advice of one veterinarian and not end his life prematurely. For the next forty-five days, I injected our Tiger with fluids and gave him pain medication every three hours. We cherished the extra time with Tiger and he let us know when it was time to let him go. Chet and I cried in each other's arms. It hurt to lose Tiger Two but we both knew that it was symbolic of what we were facing as our last team effort—Chet's death.

I told Chet over and over that I loved him even more than when we first met. I told him I was grateful for his love and it was an honor and a privilege to help care for him. Chet would have done the same thing for me. He loved me and he gave me hope when my life seemed hopeless and he helped save my life. I loved him and I gave him hope when things seemed hopeless, but I couldn't save his life.

Chester Arthur McRobert, Jr., my best friend, my husband of thirty-eight years, and the love of my life died at home on December 11, 2003. I kissed him good-bye and walked him to the hearse that was waiting by the curb in front of our house. I am so grateful for our love. We were a good team. Chet hoped to be able to play golf again and he would find it ironic that although I live on a golf course, I don't have time to play golf. My writing is a full-time job.

I will always keep Chet's favorite flowers, orchids and roses, on what I call my altar, next to the urn that holds his ashes until mine are mixed with his and together we will be partially sprinkled on Mount Hood and put to final rest at

Willamette National Cemetery. I begin and end each day at that altar. It is without a doubt, the best part of the day.

The days and nights without Chet have been a challenge. There is a hole in my heart and soul that will never heal. I wish I had recorded Chet's voice so I could "check in" with him. I miss hearing Chet's calm and soothing voice that always made me feel so loved. It's the forty years of memories we shared that keep me going—one day at a time.

It's one thing to face a loved one's death. It's quite another to face your own death. It's much easier. I faced death as a spiritual experience in 2004 from a benign cystic tumor of the pancreas. It took almost a year to get to the point that it could be diagnosed and treated. I was at peace with dying in what seemed to be a matter of weeks since my weight was approaching 100 pounds and I was losing a pound a day no matter how much I ate. I thought, "I've had a good life and when it's your time—it's your time." I called Dr. Grossnickle to tell him I wasn't going to last much longer and he said, "Let's see if we missed something." With further testing I was told that my problem was a benign pancreatic cystic tumor and it could be removed surgically.

That was an interesting point in my life choosing whether I would live or die. I chose life. It was the eighth time I cheated death. The surgery was successful. The remaining twenty per cent of my pancreas seems to be happy. I look forward to as many years as I have been allotted on this earth. As my sister, Marge, and my brother, Dean, used to say, "Life is what you make it."

I'm back to my country roots of feeding the livestock: my two cats, the birds and a squirrel that dances in gratitude. My irrigation duties are limited to the pots on my deck.

When I began to write this book, I couldn't recall the name of the restaurant where Chet and I first talked in 1960. Since it is a vital part of our story, I made a trip to Portland's Hollywood district to refresh my memory. The red traffic light that brought us together is located at an intersection less than a full block from Sandy Boulevard where Broadway Avenue begins abruptly with a very sharp curve. The curve makes it impossible to see oncoming traffic clearly from either direction until you're at the intersection. Chet could not have known that I would be stopped at that particular red traffic light going west—at precisely the same time he was stopped there going east. It was our destiny to meet. The stars were aligned.

1. Chester A. McRobert, Senior and Mr. Carr opened dealership in 1930. 2. Chester A. McRobert, Junior. Ford dealer -1973-2001. 3. Left: Marc, Bradley. Delores McRobert. 4. Chet and Gussie's wedding with Greg supervising. 5. Chet and Gussie boarding the Mauritania. 6. Cunard Line Mauretania, rust and all. 7. Chet on board. 8. View from Estoeril de Sol. 9. Chet and Gussie under the family chestnut tree.

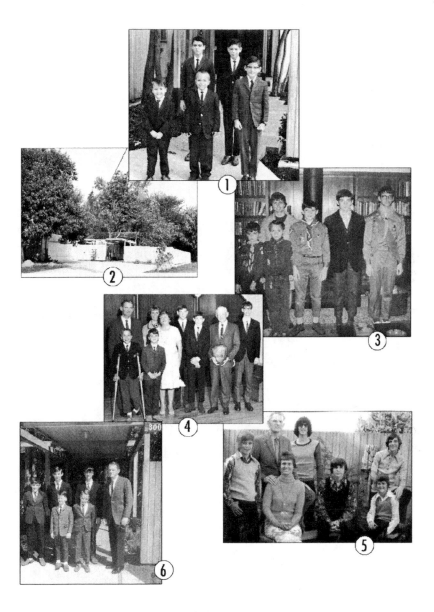

1. Front: Tim, Greg, Brad. Back: Skip, Marc. 2. Our Wallula Avenue house. 3. Front: Skip, Greg, Brad, Marc, Skip. Back: Gussie. 4. Front: Greg, Tim. Back: Chet, Gussie, Evelyn, Brad, Chester, Skip at Waverly Country Club Easter dinner. 5. Front: Gussie, Brad, Tim. Back left: Greg, Chet, Skip, Marc. 6. Front: Tim, Greg. Back left: Brad, Marc, Skip, Chet.

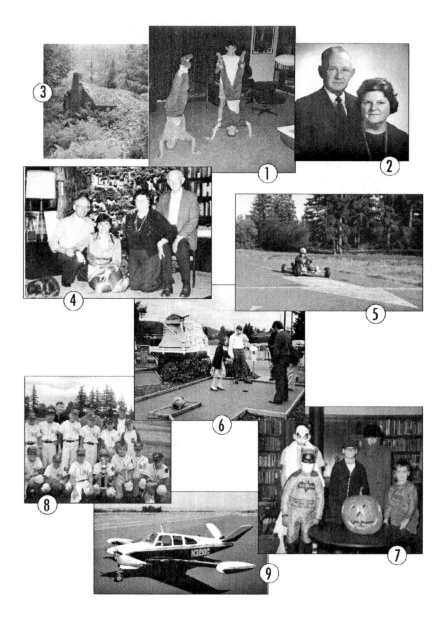

1. Greg, Brad helping Tim. 2. Chester and Evelyn McRobert. 3. Kalama River cabin rotting. 4. Chet, Gussie, Evelyn, Chester. 5. Sunday go-cart fun. 6. Heather Robertson, Marc, Brad. 7. Marc, Greg, Brad, Skip, Tim. 8. Little League, Back, Marc second from left. 9. AeroCredit Beechcraft Bonanza, Chet's second love.

1. Gussie's Pilot Logbook. 2. Proof. 3. Summer vacation in Sun Valley. 4. Brad, Greg, Marc, Tim, Chet, Skip. 5. Gussie, Chet - top of Texas, Mt. Hood Meadows. 6. Tim, Alta, Utah. 7. Chet, spring skiing, Timberline. 8. Greg, Chet, Mt. Hood Meadows South Canyon. 9. Gussie, Chet, Mt. Hood Meadows South Canyon. 10. First & last trailer of spring break vacation. 11. Skip - Eagle Scout ceremony. 12. Greg, Skip, Tim.

1. Regular visitor. 2. Quiet corner under elm tree. 3. Gussie's swimming partner. 4. Winter swimming. 5. Glamour for Chet. 6. Chet. 7. Kindel Brown's first birthday, sister Kristina Brown. 8. Kristina age three, Kindel age two. 9. Granddaughters: Kindel, Heather Robertson, Kristina Brown. 10. Heather Robertson. 11. Kindel, Kristina Brown.

1. Gussie 40 and proud. 2. Chet, Gussie. 3. Chet won $100,000 Power Ball. 4. Front: Cheryl, Kristina, Kindel Brown, Jade, Gussie, Chet, Heather, Brad. Back: Greg, Marc, Donna, Tim, Maureen, Skip, Rita. 5. Chet - Portland Japanese Garden. 6. Horishi Kuriso entry garden feature. 7. Chet, Tiger Two. 8. Gussie, Chet. 9. The T-Bird, Chet and Gussie's 35th wedding anniversary.

1. Greg, Skip, Marc, Chet, Brad, Tim and the beloved T-Bird. 2. Front: Skip, Kristina, Chet, Gussie, Kindel, Greg. Back: Marc, Donna, Suzanne, Tim, Brad, Rita, Heather. 3. Chet and his buddy.
4. Wallula squirrel. 5. Herbie, Persimmon squirrel. 6. Chet, Gussie's 38th wedding anniversary.
7. Chet's ashes.

CHAPTER NINE

WOMEN AT WORK

By the late 1960s, expectations and the role of nurses had changed. They no longer had to stand when male physicians entered the charting area or bow or duck when temperamental surgeons threw surgical instruments across the operating room. Their role had expanded beyond that of a physician's lowly handmaiden.

I enjoyed hands-on patient care, and after passing the State examination for professional registered nurses, I chose to work at Woodland Park, a small hospital close to home. Those were the days before freeways bisected communities and provided direct access from our little town to Portland Hospitals. I thought only of the convenience of the location and I admit I did not inquire about the reputation of Woodland Park Hospital.

I was assigned to critically ill patients in the days before hospitals had Intensive Care Units. But the three days a week I was supposed to work frequently ended up being extended to five days. The nurses whose work assignment was five days were expected to work seven days.

The most difficult part of working at Woodland Park Hospital at that particular time was the overabundance of quack physicians, i.e. doctors who had been kicked out of other hospitals. We had to report their patient's medical problems to our superiors and chart their symptoms and the number of times we called these doctors about their patient's complaints and problems to protect ourselves. It got so bad I couldn't sleep worrying about what mess I would find the next day.

I finally quit when I had to deal with a doctor who poked a hole through a man's urethra while he was catheterizing him with a metal instrument, and then left the hospital as though nothing had happened. I reported the incident to the head nurse who called the doctor several times and risked her job by urging him to call a specialist. I charted the details about the bloody affair and the poor man's symptoms. He had to have surgery to repair the damage done by his "physician."

The hospital administrator apparently didn't report these atrocities to the Board of Medical Examiners because the same bad apples continued to perform surgery. Surgeons complained about having to "clean up" after the quacks but in those days doctors didn't rat out other doctors.

The Board of Directors finally cleaned house and took away the quack physician's hospital privileges. Woodland Park Hospital recovered. I was a patient in the hospital on two occasions and was very satisfied with the care. But I was sad to see the hospital declare bankruptcy in 2004. Symphony Healthcare, the for-profit company that owned the facility, blamed insurance companies funded by other Portland hospitals for the closure.

If it wasn't bad doctors it was hospital administrator's trying to save money by moving registered nurses out of patient care and into administration. Nurses would become paper pushers.

It was a losing battle, so I gave up on hospitals and worked for the Oregon Children Services Division in a residential psychiatric facility for children. Chet wasn't thrilled with the night shift but I held my ground. The Child Development and Rehabilitation Center was unique in that families could accompany the child-patient and live on-site in apartments. After President Richard Nixon impounded the mental health funds, the CDRC closed and I was as distraught as the patients at its loss.

I was determined to keep my nurses license current for financial security and between the American Red Cross blood bank, my physician's office, and producing news reports on health issues I was able to do so until 1990 when my mayoral duties demanded more of my time. When I was working on Christmas day to meet a deadline, I decided enough was enough. While I had mixed feelings about the practice of nursing, there isn't a day that I don't think about how my nursing education has benefited me over the years.

Also on my list of things I needed to do was acknowledge the importance of physical activity in my life. I was a country girl used to being more physically active than city life allowed. While we jogged and walked around the neighborhood it wasn't the same as participating in an activity that required skill and made your blood race. I had skied with friends at Crater Lake north of Klamath Falls when I was in high school and since Chet was an expert skier and I loved the mountains, skiing was a good fit for me.

To me, skiing down a mountainside is a form of meditation, of being at one with the mountain. The confidence I gained from navigating down a ski slope gave me confidence to examine my life and where I was headed.

What began as just four women escaping to Mt. Hood for a day dedicated only to us evolved into the "Gresham Get Aways" and almost a hundred women traveling by bus to the Mt. Hood Meadows ski area twice a week. There were no rules except the bus left at 4 PM sharp.

My good friend Dorothy Livermore and I saw to it that beginners never went up the chairlift for the first time without an experienced skier to reassure them. If they didn't have friends to guide them down the first run, Dorothy would accompany them to the bottom. As their skiing improved with lessons some women were still leery of the steeper runs. I took them to a small but steep hill about the height of a two-story house located at the top of the Blue Chair. My theory was that if they gained confidence on the smaller hill, they could graduate to the longer, steeper Mount Hood slopes. The Gresham Get Aways had more people in the advanced classes from our two buses than Portland had with four.

We all thought we were just skiing but we changed lives. Two women divorced their husbands. Both said learning to ski increased their confidence and helped them understand they would be happier as single women. Another who hadn't been allowed to play outside as a girl because she might dirty her dress stormed down the Elevator Shaft as if it was flat. Other Get Aways including me went back to school and changed careers. Life lessons can be learned anywhere. The challenge and freedom you feel when you're flying down ski slopes feeling as if you are at one with the mountain is hard to beat.

I realized I needed a new profession. Or as my mother would have said, "What are you going to do next?" I enjoyed writing but didn't have any idea about where that could lead. It occurred to me that I needed to try something entirely out of character to look at myself differently. Something "out of the box" would be the term today. So I went to Gloria LaVonne's Modeling School.

I had no interest in becoming a model but I thought it would make me delve into myself in ways I had never experienced as a country girl. The class I enjoyed the most was the speech training. I had done well in that field in my high school days and I wondered if it might be a match with my urge to write.

I worked with Penny Avila, the instructor/speech pathologist and she urged me to consider broadcasting. As an observer of the nightly TV news programs, success in television seemed to depend too much on personal appearance to suit me. I'm not ugly but one advantage of radio is that it didn't matter what I looked like. I could just be me. Take it or leave it.

So I worked as a volunteer at the local public radio station, interviewed visiting authors and produced historical pieces about the holidays we celebrate; went back to school, and my next adventure was broadcast journalism with radio as my venue. How I looked wouldn't matter.

The number of women in broadcasting was increasing in the 1980s but most Portland stations had only a token number of women. When I interviewed for a position at KOAP-FM radio, now known as Oregon Public Broadcasting Radio, I was asked, "Are you sure you'll have enough time for this job after you do your housework?" For the life of me, I can't remember what my answer was but it must not have been too sarcastic because I was hired.

Part of my job was to create a news division in the Portland office since the only news operation for this statewide organization was miles away at Oregon State University in Corvallis. But I knew that someone was unhappy with my arrival when I saw the equipment with which I was supposed to produce broadcast-quality news reports.

My workroom was more like a closet than a production studio. Shirley Howard, a longtime public broadcasting employee and I had worked together when I was a volunteer. She was not my supervisor, but she did give me an orientation about the various departments and staff. Shirley's gig was a live interview program every morning at a Portland hotel and she was skeptical about the value of a public broadcasting news bureau in Portland. She was also somewhat skeptical of me as it turned out.

Shirley said the reel-to-reel tape recorder I would work with had been "gerry-rigged by cannibalizing three old recorders." It rested in all its glory on two thick Yellow Pages phone books. The final proof that she was not thrilled with my hiring was her glee when she showed me the box of alligator clips sitting by the recorder. She explained that I had to physically change clips each and every time I changed from editing my voice-over recordings to sound bites from meetings or news conferences.

I put up with that amateur hour production for one day and marched down stairs to the engineering department. The guys laughed and said, "We wondered how long you would put up with that." No more alligator clips. Setting me up to fail wasn't gender or age discrimination but fear of competition. That's understandable.

Shirley's explanations of how the station worked and who was responsible for what seemed more complicated than necessary. So after I spent a month at San Diego State University's KPBS public radio station, thanks to a grant from the Corporation for Public Broadcasting, I understood there were differences in how the two stations handled similar situations. I made a list of the things that just didn't make sense procedurally at KOAP.

I called department managers to ask, for example, about the procedure for checking out a company car and in each case I had been given wrong information. With confirmation that I had indeed been set up to fail, I backed Shirley Howard into a corner and with my hand on her shoulder, looking her straight in the eye, I said, "I don't know what you're up to but I'm here to stay. You tried to get me in trouble with department heads and I'm telling you now don't you *ever* do that to me again." She stopped playing her "get rid of Gussie games" and Shirley and I became friends. Her job was never at risk.

Success is the best revenge. I produced three news reports for National Public Radio (NPR) on my cannibalized, gerry-rigged tape recorder sitting on two phone books in the hall closet. I was also a weekly contributor to *Weekend West* produced by KPBS in San Diego, the prototype for what is now called Weekend Edition—Saturday. BUT NO ALLIGATOR CLIPS. NEVER AGAIN.

I hosted a weekly program called the Oregon Report for KOAP-TV and I also produced a documentary about pollution in Eastern Oregon from uranium tailings and a hazardous waste dumpsite.

The stream that provided the City of Lakeview's drinking water cut right through the middle of a huge mound of uranium tailings that made the Geiger counter sing. Lake County had the highest cancer rate in the state. The State finally covered the uranium tailings with a thick coat of soil after our publicity. What seemed beyond resolution, however, were the miles of rural roads covered with uranium tailings and left to contaminate the dust that blew across fields of sagebrush into town where it ended up in people's lungs.

As if radioactive uranium tailings weren't enough contamination for one community, there was also an abandoned hazardous waste dumpsite a few miles from town covered with a stinking pink chemical brew that you could smell miles away. It was near an upwelling artesian spring.

State officials believed strongly that the spring's pressure was high enough to prevent the stinking mess between the rows of chemical gravesites from contaminating the spring. I predicted that the farmers having to dig deeper wells and lowering the water table would adversely affect the spring's upwelling pressure. They countered that it would never happen.

Unfortunately, I was right and they were wrong. The spring's pressure dropped drastically giving the pink poisonous chemicals access to the aquifer that was a major source of drinking water for Lakeview residents.

KKSN-AM was an upstart radio station in the Portland market and was closely watched by the Federal Communications Commission (FCC). Formerly known as KISN-AM, the station was forced to close in the 1970s after Senator Mark Hatfield filed a complaint that the station had not provided his campaign the same amount of airtime it had given to his challenger.

My friend, Martha Bergman, was applying for a job at KKSN-AM and I went with her out of curiosity. David Smith, the News Director wanted to produce an hour and a half morning drive-time news cast called 91 Northwest with longer news pieces than those heard on most commercial stations. It would be similar to public broadcasting news programs so Dave was interested in hiring Martha and me. I was skeptical and didn't sign on at first. I wondered whether a public broadcasting format could succeed on commercial radio. But the more I thought about it the more I liked the idea. I called Dave, "Can we start over?" Long story short is that I was hired and it was a blast.

Dave was innovative and had good instincts about possible news reports. For example, he called me at 5:00 AM to cover a rally in honor of John Lennon's death. The group holding the rally didn't get a permit from the City of Portland and the Police Bureau had the impossible job of seeing that nobody honored John Lennon. The police officer in charge didn't expect me to get a microphone close enough so he could be heard telling them to move out. The crowd didn't move an inch and he relented. How could he possibly close a tribute to John Lennon?

We covered demonstrations led by the Black United Front about school desegregation issues, salmon festivals for Columbia River Indian tribes, the usual political beats, as well as women's issues.

Dr. Alice Armstrong was organizing Portland's professional women and wanted them to know that just ten years earlier, in 1971, Oregon men could commit their wives to mental hospitals for just about anything that displeased them. An Oregon man had his wife committed to Dammasch State Hospital for "burning the potatoes." That was the only offense listed on the commitment order.

She was an educated professional woman who had worked for many years, and became depressed when she married and was expected to be a stay-at-home housewife. Dr. Armstrong was then a psychologist in resident training at the hospital and brought her patient a typewriter as part of her therapy. She was severely chastised for her actions. Her superiors ordered her to remove the offensive typewriter from the patient's room and limit her therapy to learning how to cook without burning the potatoes.

Dr. Armstrong refused and she was fired. That was the same year the Supreme Court ruled that women were indeed "persons" with the same legal standing as men. It came too late for the woman who burned the potatoes.

I have not done a study to prove that being straightforward and honest with people builds trust but my experience shows that truth and trust are partners. Even if you have to say something people don't want to hear I've found it's better to say it like it is. An incident with a public official while I was at KKSN-AM confirmed my theory.

I covered a story about several white police officers charged with throwing dead opossums in front of a restaurant owned by a man who was black. It had created a firestorm across the city. Portland Commissioner Charles Jordan was in charge of the Police Department and had called a news conference. Commissioner Jordan and I were on good terms. Before his election I gave him some information that was helpful so we had a beginning base of trust.

The Commissioner had scheduled a news conference to deal with the "possum" issue as it was being called around the city. I was early, but I saw him in a conference room with some people so I opened the door, walked in, and started recording the meeting. The Commissioner said, "Hello, Gussie" but it wasn't until sometime later that he mentioned the meeting was a briefing not the news conference. He just asked that I not record some of the discussion and I agreed. Later we also agreed that I would not air what was said at the meeting until after the investigation was completed and disciplinary actions would then be announced.

Looking back at this incident, the Commissioner must have seen me as someone he could trust. If I said I wouldn't air the private discussion he could count on it not being on the evening news.

When the investigation was completed, Commissioner Jordan called me and basically said, "Go for it." News Director Dave was pleased about KKSN-AM scooping all the other Portland stations with a report that included more in-depth information than they were reporting. I wouldn't have had the 'story behind the story' if Commissioner Jordan hadn't trusted me.

David Smith's version of the news won top honors from the Oregon Associated Press at the annual awards ceremony our first year on the air. He and his duo anchor, Gina Tuttle, my fellow reporter, Lester Friedman and I received an Associated Press (AP) award for KKSN Brave News Radio. The Oregon A.P. cited KKSN-AM's News Department for its "very professional and factual yet conversational approach to the news." It hangs on my office wall today along with my press pass. I couldn't believe I got paid for work that was so much fun.

I have always been interested in health issues, but my special interest in the physical effects of sulfur and sulfiting agents used as food whiteners and preservatives began on Sunday morning, May 18, 1980.

I was at the KKSN-AM studio just south of the Columbia River on N.E. 158th Avenue doing a live interview with the manager of the Oregon Hazardous Waste Division. The interview went well with very candid answers to my questions about the Lakeview problems and a landfill that was oozing chemicals into a Hood River County stream killing the fish. Then my nose started gushing like a fire hydrant. That was my first, but unfortunately not my last, reaction to the millions of tons of sulfur dioxide spewed skyward by the eruption of Mount Saint Helen. My lungs filled with fluid and I didn't breathe, I gurgled.

So much so that while Chet and I were waiting at the SeaTac airport in Seattle for a flight to Portland one day, people moved across the room wondering if I was going to explode. It seemed to me that certain foods made it worse: lettuce and cut fruit at salad bars and any dried herb that was suspiciously bright green. Peppermint tea brought on the SeaTac episode.

In desperation, I called Dr. Lendon Smith, a controversial, ahead-of-his-time Portland physician. He suggested taking Vitamin A daily. I was grateful to be able to breathe without gurgling. Later, with a list of products and foods that contained sulfites from the Center For Science In The Public Interest (CSPI), I could get by without the extra Vitamin A.

I was also doing research for an article in the Food Day section of *The Oregonian* and I put a small classified ad in the Public Notice section of the newspaper asking people to contact me if they had "health problems from sulfite preservatives in salad bars and processed foods." Responses came from as far away as New York City and Canyon Lake, California, as well as Oregon and Washington. One included a letter written to the MGM Grand Hotel's manager in Reno, Nevada to report an incident of acute respiratory failure that had required a 911 call and a trip to the hospital. I shared the "magical sulfite list" with everyone who responded.

That ended the daily and deadly walk through the sulfite minefields for those of us who lack a liver enzyme that changes sulfites to sulfates. With the Center for Science in the Public Interest list we could for the first time avoid sulfites.

Sulfites were widely used as color enhancers and preservatives on fresh fruits and vegetables and fortunately those uses are now banned. Sulfites occur naturally in some foods and are also created during fermentation in processed foods. Allergy specialists can help point out which foods to avoid.

Dried fruit that retains its natural color and herbs that look suspiciously green have been treated with sulfites or sulfur dioxide and can cause respiratory problems. Sulfites are used to condition commercial bread dough and to lengthen the shelf life of some medications. It is also used as a whitener in gelatin. When I asked pharmaceutical company representatives whether their capsules contained sulfites, the answer was, "No."

A more accurate answer would be that while sulfites are not added in the production of individual capsules it is used as a whitener at what I call the bone factory where they grind and boil bones, tendons, and the skin of slaughtered animals to produce gelatin. It would be an icky grey color without sulfites. I won't take a chance on any capsule even though the pharmaceutical and supplement industries promote them as easier to digest. They are, of course, safe for those people fortunate enough to not be sensitive to sulfites.

Those who are not as fortunate can suffer from severe respiratory problems including asthma. Other symptoms include dizziness, sweating and feeling hot, vomiting, and anaphylactic shock, which can result in death if not treated quickly after exposure. Some people have experienced spikes in blood pressure and not being able to sleep. They were "too wired."

Instead of the Oregonian Food Day sulfites article, I wrote a front-page news article about ten year old Medaya McPike's death caused by anaphylactic shock after ingesting sulfites contained in guacamole and lettuce at a restaurant salad bar, and how the Director of the Oregon Health Department had disregarded three Federal Drug Administration (FDA) warnings and was heavily influenced by the food processing and restaurant lobby.

Representative Ron Wyden (D-Oregon) told me he used the article as a "template" as he and Senator Al Gore (D-Tennessee) drafted H.R. 1427. The anti–sulfite-ban lobby gave up and supported the Wyden/Gore bill that was presented to Congress seven days after Medaya McPike died.

The Ninety-Ninth Congress answered the question frequently asked by Michael Jacobson of the Center for Science in the Public Interest—"How many sulfite deaths are acceptable?" The answer was "Zero" and the FDA was forced to act responsibly saving thousands of lives.

When I open a bag of salad greens I look for the "No preservatives" claim, which is code for no sulfites, and give thanks for the work of Congressman Wyden and Senator Gore in 1985.

The fun was over and KKSN-AM closed not from Mt. St. Helens or lack of an audience but from management trading advertisement revenue for personal services that didn't pay the station's bills. When the Internal Revenue Service padlocked the doors and put up signs saying that until the taxes were paid, the padlocks were permanent fixtures not even David Smith's magic could resolve the problem.

So I jumped ship to KGW-AM Radio. My 52-seconds long *It's Your Health* public service pieces played regularly on this popular station. I also worked as a news reporter and Chet's inside knowledge of some financial problems plaguing Portland's regional government gave me another scoop. While KGW-

AM was always one of the top rated Portland stations the Seattle based owner closed the station to the dismay of its many listeners. This was the beginning of the end for many AM stations with FM frequency becoming more popular.

While there were fewer women than men in broadcasting in Portland, I did not experience gender discrimination at KOAP once I got past the job interview or later at KKSN-AM and KGW-AM. I was just a girl who was used to being treated as an equal by the boys from the time I could walk. Somehow that must resonate in me.

I then put together my Rx Radio News Network of sixty Oregon stations to air the public service announcements and commercials I produced for non-profit organizations and government agencies.

I was unaware that the Oregon State Bar had applied for national awards for a series of public service announcements that I had written and produced to celebrate the Bicentennial of the U. S. Constitution. I was happy to say the least when the series won two national awards in 1987: The Spotlight Award, "First Place Award for Radio Public Service Announcements" from the Public Relations Society of America, and the Gold Circle Award from the American Society of Association Executives. It felt good!

I expanded my Rx Radio News Network and produced a syndicated radio series called *Tune In To Health*. The series was well received by a national syndications company and station program managers in three states and Calgary, Canada, but a nationwide recession severely decreased corporate advertising revenue, and radio stations were closing across the country. *Tune In To Health's* future was uncertain until United Press International asked for exclusive broadcast rights. The contract was actually in the mail when UPI declared bankruptcy. It had everything to do with timing.

1. Registered Nurse Gussie McRobert at graduation. 2. Mt. Hood Meadows Day Lodge. 3. Gresham Get Aways. 4. Ready to go. 5. Almost there. 6. The view is beautiful. 7. Get Aways headed down the mountain.

1. Gussie and Rene Farwig ready to ski 2. Ringleaders Gussie and Dorothy Livermore. 3. Gussie's KOAP Press Pass. 4. KKSN AP Award for Best News Program. 5. Gussie gets a Master's Degree. 6. News Director David Smith and anchor Gina Tuttle. 7. KKSN Press Pass.

When one door closes another door does in fact open. I covered local government news as a reporter for KOAP, KKSN and KGW radio stations and spent sixteen years as a volunteer on parks and land use committees. It wasn't that much of a stretch to run for City Council of Gresham, a small city of 60,000 people—even if I was a woman. A city department director urged me to run, but I had to check out the building for chemicals, mold, etc. The walls in the room where Council meetings were held were raw concrete and could be a problem. So I sat in the room for an hour and didn't itch or fade so I passed Round One.

On to Round Two: I had seen the good side of government, but it seemed to me that you had to sell your soul to the devil of politics to get elected, and then do it again every day to stay in office. Still, I felt I could do a good job if I didn't let all that get in the way.

It was now Round Three: I wouldn't take on a commitment like that without talking with Chet. After a joint Chet/Gussie decision that I would run for a City Council seat, I stood in front of the mirror in my dressing room, looked myself straight in the eye, and made a vow to myself that if I was elected I would not take that First Step. The one that would make the Second Step easier, and then the Third and Fourth Steps taken without hesitation into the murky swampland of buying and selling politicians.

My motivation to run for office was to replace a City Council whose role was basically to serve the City Manager, Wally Douthwaite. City government was a top-down technocracy starting with, of course, the City Manager, then his staff, followed by a City Council that did what they were told to do. There was absolutely no opportunity for citizens to be involved in the decisions that affected their lives and bank accounts. They were not allowed to see staff reports until the night of the City Council meetings when it was too late to make changes. The mayor's favorite saying was, "We'll cram it down their throats." Douthwaite told me, "Staff thinks you ask too many questions."

He was a technocrat with a capital T. That is "Staff knows absolutely positively what's best for you and everybody else. Stay out of our way, and most importantly, don't ask questions."

The crystallizing moment when I said "enough is enough" was the City Council meeting that we hoped would finalize the city's approval of a building permit allowing the Gresham Historical Society to remodel an historic church. The Historical Society had hoped to use it for weddings. The meeting ended with insults instead of resolution.

City planners would give the Historical Society ten hoops to jump through and then ten more and ten more and so on. It was clear our elected officials hoped the Society would give up in defeat. I was so angry I said, "I just might run for City Council."

While I was still standing after Round Three, I got absolutely no support to run for a Council seat. What everyone said was, "We need a mayor!" I talked to several previous mayors and they all said the same thing, "Go for it. The mayor's job is entirely different."

Round Four led to comparing the personal aspects of being a mayor or a councilor. So it was back to talks with Chet about how both positions would affect our personal lives. Even with Gresham's Council/Manager form of government in which elected officials are limited to policy making and administration is the job of the manager, the mayor's job would be more time consuming than the councilor's.

Chet favored a run for mayor. He had run unsuccessfully for mayor and lost because so many people thought he was a shoo-in that they didn't bother to vote. Chet was not interested in running again and he, too, said, "Go for it!" So I went for it! I filed a notice with the City Recorder that I intended to be a candidate for mayor in the November 1988 election.

I was following in the footsteps of my father-in-law, Chet, Sr., who was a City Councilor and my husband, Chet, Jr. who served on the Planning Commission for fourteen years. Their leadership style was similar to mine. Get people together and talk things out. The issues become clear and the solutions then have the support of the people who will live with them.

I had a year to attend meetings and get up to speed on issues. So I put together a team of advisors for the campaign who then became my kitchen cabinet after I was elected. There wasn't a day I didn't reach for my McHelper's List and call people to talk about issues facing the City.

I annoyed the committee at first because I wanted the campaign to be based on a marketing plan that took me longer to produce than some thought was necessary. When it was finally completed, my finance guru, Jim Hood, said, "We could use it to conquer Normandy." We set our sights on Gresham instead and when the campaign got mean at the end, as I knew it would, we simply "worked the plan," and stayed on track. I was elected by a margin of three to one over two male opponents, one of whom was mayor.

The man the voters rejected had been known as a "rubber stamp" mayor. The City Manager repeated his concern about me, "Staff still thinks you ask too many questions." I said, "Get used to it."

Newspaper articles had speculated for weeks about whether the new U. S. Bank Operations Center would be built in Oregon or Washington. Gresham was on the list to gain the bank's 1,000 new jobs so the first question I asked on my very first day as mayor was, "Where are we with the U. S. Bank project?" Mr. Douthwaite's response was, "They know where we are." In other words, he was doing absolutely nothing to promote our city.

So I called Roger Breezley, CEO of U. S. Bank to pitch Gresham, and I also called the State Economic Development Department and asked for help. Governor Neil Goldschmidt was determined those thousand jobs would come to Oregon, not Washington across the Columbia River, so it became a priority for the State specialists. They had to drag City staff to the table kicking and screaming, but with the strong support of four of seven Councilors, they eventually gave up and cooperated. State officials kept them from sabotaging the deal.

Staff thought the elected City Council should show up, keep quiet, and vote as they were told. The previous Council didn't receive information about the issues they would be voting on until the Friday before their Tuesday meeting so if they wanted to spend time with family and friends during the weekend, they came unprepared for the Council meeting—and did exactly what the staff wanted them to do. They never questioned a staff report. I did question staff reports and I was chastised. The City Manager's assistant said, "You have no business questioning staff's judgment." It made me wonder what they were hiding.

The new Council changed the hands off, keep them dumb process to "we will help develop Council Business Items from the beginning and we want the people who pay the City's bills, the taxpayers, at the table with us." The battle began in earnest when we refused to take action on a land use issue because the staff report was not based on facts. It rambled on with scenarios that could not be substantiated and did not address the pertinent legal issues.

We demanded accurate and professional reports on which to make our Council decisions. They were to be based on City policies and codes instead of make believe scenarios. Outrage was instant and spread like wild fire through the cubicles and offices of the staff. They were used to serving the technocracy instead of the public and the City Council.

With the help of a friend who was a Portland land use attorney, I drafted staff reports opposing City staff development proposals that did not meet City Code. When the new Council wanted changes staff did not support, I documented the need for change and the benefits for presentation at the next meeting.

We added a Council Business Item for Councilors to bring up issues at Council meetings that needed to be addressed. Under the old system, the elected officials chosen by voters to represent them could not bring up new issues for discussion at a Council meeting or any other time. That violated the rubber stamp rule that staff always knows what is best for everyone.

It was nuclear level war. While there were some City employees who actually wanted to work for the public they had to lay low. If the issue was whether the American flag was red, white, and blue, and the four new Council members voted yes, the three carryovers would vote no. At a goal setting session, one of the carryovers, the blonde bomber, said, "We don't want economic development. It makes too much work for the staff." Mr. Douthwaite shook his head in agreement. Rumors around town were that the manager's friend's projects went to the top of the application pile. The uppity newcomers made the manager's friends get in line like everyone else.

The manager was more than a little angry with the mayor and the three newly elected Councilors who supported working with and for the community. Douthwaite and most, but not all of his staff, didn't support the changes we campaigned for and were elected to implement. We had to change the way the City did business.

I was naïve enough to think, "They're professionals. They wouldn't do anything to hurt the City." I was dead wrong. That was absolutely the most important business for department directors. Years later, I learned it was Job One.

The City Manager appointed department directors to organize and implement a "Make Enough Trouble to Get Rid of the Four Newcomers Committee" whose only charge was to think of ways to disrupt City services. Their assignment was to create such a mess that Gresham voters would fire the Mayor and the three Councilors who often voted with her in the next election.

Fortunately, there were some true public servants who alerted me to the City Manager's plan. One of his strategies was to delay critical street improvements that would bring construction in a particularly fast-growing area of the city to a halt. At a budget meeting soon after the heads-up phone calls, I leafed through pages of the Transportation Department's budget trying to look puzzled as I asked, "Where are the improvements for 182nd and Powell? I know they're here somewhere but new that I am, I can't find them."

The City Manager's face turned as red as a ripe tomato and he yelled at the staff to find them. Of course, nobody could find the missing item and the City Manager was caught with his campaign strategy pants at half-mast. The Council and Budget Committee voted to include the project for funding. The City Manager's games continued until I got three votes in addition to my own to fire him.

With the support of citizens and business groups, we rammed a community visioning process through the Budget Committee to give the people who lived in Gresham the opportunity to say what their city should look like when "it grew up." We called it Envision Gresham-2020 and people of all ages participated in the year long process. School children decorated the Council chambers with posters, collages, and essays about pollution, homelessness, recycling, drugs, and crime. They were the same concerns we heard from adults.

Implementing the vision required public investment, but since citizens knew what they were buying they approved bond measures for parks, the first open space acquisition program in the state to purchase and preserve our many buttes, creek corridors, and almost a thousand acres of natural areas. And they didn't flinch when utility rates were increased to help with water and sewer infrastructure maintenance.

While I was an advocate of growth and "smart development," I didn't want the city paved over with asphalt, so I initiated the first voter-approved open space rescue and trail development program in Oregon. More than 700 acres of buttes, watersheds, wetlands, and creek corridors have been preserved, and 55 miles of off-road trails developed for recreation and off-road transportation.

Now, no matter which City issue I occasionally mouth off about some City staff and/or their spouses write letters to the editor of the local newspaper saying that I was a disaster as mayor. That's code for the technocrats "we know what's best for you" staffers were NOT in charge of the City when Gussie was mayor. The taxpayers came first and if I said I was going to do something, they could count on me to keep my word. I kept a record of those promises and checked them off one by one.

The first challenge to my First Step promise to myself to avoid getting sucked into shady politics was a bond-rating trip to New York City. The City Manager would always walk right by me without speaking. So we didn't discuss the trip, and other than what little the office staff told me about reservations and small details, I didn't know quite what to expect when we got there. The city manager, finance director, a local businessman, and I were to represent the City of Gresham along with a respected bond counsel.

The first night in New York, we met to go over our presentations, which we hoped would result in getting the City a good bond rating. The meeting with Moody's and Standard and Poor the next day went well and our mission to get lower interest costs for Gresham taxpayers was successful.

I was pleased with the outcome of my first trip to New York City as mayor until our bond counsel took us out to celebrate at a swanky restaurant followed by a Broadway play. The hundred-dollar bottle of wine was good—not exquisite. The steak I had was almost as good as Klamath County beef, but more expensive. Although it was the middle of winter, fresh asparagus and raspberries were ordered without concern for the extravagant price. Instead of retuning to Portland the next day with the rest of the group, I went on to Washington, D.C. to lobby our Congressional delegation about City issues.

Back in Gresham, my first item of business was to ask the office staff exactly how the costs of the trip were handled. Specifically, I wanted to know the procedure to pay for the amount that was above the average cost of a New York City dinner as well as the Broadway play and the wine. I knew there was a City policy against using taxpayer money for alcohol and the play was an obvious no-no.

The response was dead silence. Then as word spread about my concerns, the Finance Director and bond counsel quickly assured me that the dinner, the play, and the expensive bottle of wine didn't cost the City anything extra. I thought "and other fairy tales" and countered that the costs had to be covered in the consulting fee paid by the City and Gresham taxpayers. No company would last long paying out those kinds of freebies. They continued their hopeless task of trying to convince me that I just didn't understand how the game was played.

They must have thought I had just fallen off a Klamath Falls potato truck. I told them firmly that I was going to pay for the costs over and above an average New York City dinner, the ticket to the Broadway play, and my share of the wine. I called the restaurant to get the correct charges. In the meantime, the bond counsel dummied up a phony bill that wasn't close to the real cost. I sent her company a check for $147.50 as my share of the extravaganza.

And then all hell broke loose. The businessman who accompanied us on the trip assured me that this was just the way "it" was done. The City Manager's neighbor and Rotary Club buddy, who was also the publisher of the local newspaper, saw to it that I got hammered with headlines and articles claiming I was just a neophyte and didn't understand the world of finance. The wife of a Multnomah County employee chewed me out at a garden store, "You're making something out of nothing." So then I knew that Multnomah County staff also got sweetheart deals from their bond counsel.

I refused to play their "keep her dumb" game. My mother's advice years before came in handy, "If the shoe doesn't fit, don't put it on." The taxpayers of Gresham weren't fooled by the headlines and called to say "thanks for standing up for us." I felt good. I could look myself straight in the eye in my dressing room mirror and say I hadn't taken that First Step into the murky swamp of buying and selling politicians.

The incident made me question how important perks were to staff in charge of selecting consultants. Did the consultant who offered the most goodies get more contracts? The City Council passed a resolution that all expenses in consulting trips and local business had to be itemized. That ended the sweetheart deals at least while I was at City Hall.

The "you ask too many questions" manager told a friend after I was elected that "She's just a housewife and nothing to worry about." He was the youngest of four sons in a military family and I was old enough to be his mother. I mentioned that we had the critical quorum number to fire the city manager to a mutual friend who I knew would carry the firing message to the manager. He didn't let me down. The manager resigned before we could fire him. I hope Mr. Douthwaite learned not to mess with a female who doesn't care what he thinks when it comes to cheating taxpayers.

There is one major issue I wish I had handled differently as Mayor. It took me far too long to catch on to the "keep her dumb" game played by Tom Walsh, General Manager of the Portland Metropolitan Transit Agency (TRI-MET). Congress had approved the money for a new program to help transit agencies be financially self-sufficient. It was called Project Break Even: Transit agencies could buy, develop, and lease property for income in addition to ridership fares.

The first project was to begin on eighty-five acres adjacent to Gresham City Hall in 1989. However, the top federal transit agency staff person in charge of the Break Even program hated it and he absolutely refused to write a check to TRI-MET for $14.5 million. Nobody, not even, our Congressional delegation could change his mind.

Congress had appropriated the $14.5 million, however, and it was earmarked for Gresham projects only. When I brought it up several times, Walsh always had a reason for not moving forward. First it was because the legal firm occasionally used by TRI-MET was also the firm working with one of our Senators who had unfortunately had a one time only lapse in ethics. Then it was something else and something else and finally a warning NOT to bring it up ever again with Senator Mark Hatfield. Walsh found out I had written the Senator and asked for his help.

However, City representatives always lobbied their Congressional delegation after attending the yearly National League of Cities meeting in Washington, D.C. So Councilors Keathley, Giusto, Eichner, and I met with Senator Hatfield whose staff also warned us against talking about our $14.5 million.

So I did what any mayor would do. I asked the Senator, " When can we expect the check?" My question brought out a side of Senator Hatfield that I suspect few people have seen. His face turned purple and he erupted like a volcano, "Hasn't TRI-MET taken care of Gresham yet?" When the answer was, "No, TRI-MET hasn't taken care of Gresham" he called the same staff person who had issued the warning earlier to keep our mounts shut about our $14.5 million and told him to "make it happen."

And there is no doubt that what goes around comes around. As we left the meeting, I was overjoyed to see who was waiting to meet with Senator Hatfield. TRI-MET Manager Tom Walsh and Portland City Commissioner Earl Blumenauer were next in line. By the time we arrived back at our hotel there was a phone call from Earl the Pearl, as he is sometimes called, asking "When can we meet?" Councilor Giusto and I had dinner with them and neither of us budged an inch or gave up a penny.

The $14.5 million paid for double tracking sections of our East Side Light Rail that were only served by a single track, some street improvements, and a parking structure in our Historic Downtown.

I insisted that we receive our verbal agreement in writing as soon as we returned and they barely met the deadline we gave them. But every penny was accounted for and our little know-nothing town prevented the TRI-MET and City of Portland hotshots from transferring $14.5 million to the proposed West Side Light Rail project that would link the East Side and Portland rail system to rapidly growing Washington County. That was the reason for the stall.

I vote for Earl the Pearl, but it's with clenched teeth because at the end of the transit dollar day, then Commissioner Blumenauer, now Congressman Blumenauer was more interested in funding a new and much fancier light rail project in another county than fixing the flaws in ours.

Gresham had Sister City relationships with Ebetsu City, Japan and Sokcho City, Korea. Ebetsu is near Sapporo on Hokkaido Island, has a population of about 100,000 people, and a diverse economy with several colleges and universities. It is also known as a "Ceramics" City, the center of the bricks industry since the 1800's and is also famous for its pottery and glass crafts. Every spring, streets are cordoned off and bricks by the thousands are stood on end winding back and forth to the beginning. Everyone waits quietly in anticipation of the order to push the first brick, which sets off a magic chain of bricks falling gracefully, pushing the one in front until the several block long array has fallen at exactly the proper time and place. A Japanese delegation set up a smaller version of the Ebetsu event in Gresham's Main City Park and my granddaughter, Kindel Brown, had the honor of pushing the first brick. That brick is proudly displayed with other Asian treasures in my living room. The major concern of Ebetsu City when we visited in 1997 was having to raise revenue since the federal money that funded all Japanese cities was being cut and would likely end.

Sokcho City is in the northeast corner of South Korea on the coast of the Sea of Japan. On our 1997 visit in, we were fortunate to be in Sockcho City for the six-week long "opening" of the beaches. The rest of the year the beautiful white sand beaches were off limits with chain-link fences to prevent North Korean saboteurs from entering the country. When we drove to the Demilitarized Zone, I commented on the beautiful concrete arches that graced the two-lane highway. I was told the arches were filled with explosives to destroy the road if the North Koreans invaded South Korea. Living with the underlying but constant fear of invasion by enemy forces didn't seem to dampen our Korean hosts enthusiasm for life. Surrounded by the beauty of the Seorak-san National Park with its rocky mountain peaks reaching up to the heavens and soaking in the nearby carbonic acid hot springs must provide solace and relief from that underlying reality.

President Eisenhower established the Sister City program to prevent another world war. That was before satellite communication with instant worldwide news coverage, and the Internet. As people learned more about other countries, interest in our Sister Cities program has decreased.

Despite that fact, a City planner from Nigeria adeptly orchestrated adding a third Sister City, Owerri, Nigeria, with a population of 363,300 people. A Gresham Sister City delegation visited Owerri in 1991. I have to admit I was surprised at the interest and government support of the arts. We were amazed at student's work at the Mbari Arts and Cultural Center. Magnificent ebony carvings were on display in every small town and large city.

The timing of our visit was magical. Nigeria's military dictator wanted to change the government to a democracy. We met Chief MKO Abiola who won the election for president in 1993. The military dictator declared the election invalid and put Chief Abiola in prison. Portland Nigerians said it was because Chief Abiola was from the south and he was Muslim with more than one wife. There were limits to what the military dictators would allow in the new Nigerian democracy.

The real reason for adding Owerri as a Sister City became clear on our last day in Nigeria when we visited the American Ambassador in Lagos, William Lacy Swing. The City planner wanted me to sign the second page of a letter to Ambassador Swing. I said, "Not before I know what is on the first page." Page one clarified the true intent of the planner. It was a scam!

The instigator from Nigeria had me promising to "accept all financial and housing support" for eighteen of his brothers, sisters, and cousins. My answer was to rip both pages in half and give him a look that should have made his hair stand up like he had been struck by the spectacular sheet-lightening displays that streak across the Nigerian sky every night.

I talked to Chief Abiola twice during the election campaign. He planned to stop over in Portland on his way to Seattle to order airplanes from Boeing for his two aviation companies, Sierra-Leone and Concord Airlines, and he wanted to meet Portland business leaders.

Chief Abiola's varied business interests reflected the average Nigerian's reluctance to concentrate on just one field that might fall out of favor with a new leader in the next coup-de-tat takeover. The Chief earned a degree in business in Scotland and he founded companies in sixty countries on five continents including newspaper and magazine publishing, banking, fisheries, farming, shipping, and in partnership with Harris Communications of USA, he founded Radio Communications (Nig) Ltd.

It made perfect sense to introduce him to Portland business leaders. I made some calls and reserved a private room at the University Club after gaining assurance that Abiola's colorful Nigerian Chief's robes would not be a problem. He called later to cancel the meeting because of his presidential campaign.

Chief Moshood Kasimawo Olawale Abiola died in prison in 1998 from a heart attack just one day before he was to be released. His lovely wife, Alhaja

Kudirat Abiola, who served us tea in their Lagos home was shot in the head on a busy street in broad daylight in Lagos on June 4,1996.

CNN newscasters told the world about both of their deaths, but Mrs. Kuridat Abiola's brazen execution with her small red car pulled over to the curb, the door on the driver's side still open, providing the background for the entire CNN news report haunts me to this day.

Ambassador Swing said he thought Nigeria "had the best chance of success of any African country because of the innovative genius of everyday citizens." The country seems to be in continuous chaos with yet one more military dictatorship. Our hope for Nigeria ended with Chief MKO Abiola's death.

Back at City Hall, our second City Manager, Michael Casey presented the Council with a budget fifty-three percent higher than the previous year that didn't balance without a ten percent tax increase. That didn't come close to the problems faced by Sokcho City, but in Gresham it was a major problem.

Casey's blackmail budget included a 400 percent increase in "Other Professional Services" which I learned would continue ballet lessons he had approved for a female staffer. "Other Consulting Services" were up 100 percent and "Other Contractual Services" up 96 percent. Casey had no Plan B so when we said, "NO, READ OUR LIPS, NO," he expected us to eventually fold, and told staff, "Let them figure it out."

So that's exactly what we did. The Budget Committee and Council met in groups small enough to avoid violating quorum laws (Oregon budget law requires cities with fewer than 100,000 people to have a Budget Committee with an equal number of elected and unelected members). We cut $379,00 and balanced the budget without Casey's proposed ten percent increase.

We eliminated positions, froze salaries, froze purchase of new vehicles until we could approve a City policy on cars, limited the number of professional association memberships, and reduced every line item in the budget. The budget document was prepared on my Macintosh computer without hiring a single consultant. The file for the "Casey Budget Fiasco" is almost three inches high.

The staff was not particularly pleased with our effort but the taxpayers cheered. Since there was concern that the amateur's cuts were too drastic, we urged departments to bring any necessary adjustments to the Council throughout the year for approval. How many adjustments were brought forward? The answer is, "ZERO."

I didn't want another blackmail budget so I suggested that the unelected members of the Budget Committee become a year-round Finance Committee and help put the budget together. It works! No more surprises.

For the remaining five years I was mayor, the Council approved the percentage of any budget increase based on our Financial Policies and forecasts in September. Staff then had until April to get a proposed budget to us with final approval no later than the middle of June. When I left, that practice ended.

Our third City Manager, Bonnie Kraft didn't consider the Council her enemy and our relationship with staff improved. The Council, i.e., six councilors and the mayor gave clear direction and she and her staff implemented our policies. Let me be clear that policy directions were always based on the decisions of all seven elected officials—not just the mayor. It's called "cloaking yourself in the power and protection of the group."

It was not as Bonnie would later say that I had my "foot in the middle of her back" or that I made her "join the Rotary Club." So at least on the surface, we worked as a team, and that team included the public, the people who paid the bills. They served on committees and were our eyes and ears in the community.

We worked as a team and that team included the public, the people who paid the bills. They served on committees and were our eyes and ears in the community. We did good things together.

I wasn't surprised by Ms. Kraft's anti-Gussie comments. She was one who tried to convince me that the City bond counsel splurging on $150 per person dinners and $100 bottles of wine in New York City was not an ethical problem, and that the bill wasn't passed on to our taxpayers. She was by far the best of the three City managers that served during my ten years in office. I am not a fan of the Council Manager form of government.

One of our finest moments was when our little town beat some major league competitors for an economic development project. LSI Logic had narrowed its choices to expand in Austin, Texas or Gresham, Oregon. LSI Logic's CEO, Will Corrigan, and Vice President, Joe Zalayeta, asked officials from both cities to tour their California facility.

The very next day, we were in Milpitas touring and talking. Because we made the effort, Will Corrigan chose Gresham and we clobbered Austin and our competitors Governor George W. Bush and his friend, Ross Perot.

I was re-elected twice without opposition so the people who mattered most to me, the taxpayers and voters, thought I was on the right track even as our population had increased from 60,000 to almost 100,000. People stopped me in the middle of the street with horns honking and in the aisles of grocery stores to tell me the equivalent of, "I don't always agree with you but I appreciate knowing where you stand." What can I say? That's just my Henley upbringing.

Some say it's wonderful and others say it's dreadful, but it is the only one of its kind in the WORLD. That would be the twenty-five cities, three counties, and twenty-seven special service districts in the Portland metropolitan area that deal with growth management and transportation issues as a unified region. "It" is the Metropolitan Service District (METRO) and serves a combined population of 1.3 million people.

METRO had the authority to do regional land use planning but didn't pursue "We're here to help," top-down planning. They knew it would fail. I had experience with that style of planning and agreed it would be disastrous.

I served on the Multnomah County Planning Commission with staff that thought people were smart enough to participate in planning their neighborhoods. But previous County staff had taken shiny, bound copies to community meetings with no chance for the public to make even small changes.

None of us knew about that history when we naively scheduled a meeting on Sauvie Island in western Multnomah County. We barely escaped with our lives. An angry mob rushed us and if there hadn't been a door to the outside close by I don't know what would have happened to us, but I know it wouldn't have been pleasant.

Two Deputy Sheriffs with holstered guns went with us to the next three meetings and by then the Sauvie Island folks understood that it was a new game with different people and we really did want to know what they thought about growth on their home turf—they said protect our farms and that's the way it is to this day. Sauvie Island is where city people go to buy wonderful fresh fruit and vegetables.

I vowed I would NEVER be part of a "we know what's best for you" top down planning process for anything. That's the strong belief and attitude that I brought to the table as we began planning the future of the Portland metropolitan region.

Since twenty-four cities (another city has since been added) and three counties in the Portland metropolitan area share a common and troubled air shed and an urban growth boundary, it was clear something had to be done to coordinate efforts to control growth or the farmland in the Willamette Valley, one of the most productive agricultural areas in the country, would be paved over with asphalt.

So the first year I was mayor, METRO put together a committee to look at a new way of doing business. I was the pariah on the committee when I asked, yet again, too many questions. I wanted to know exactly who would do what to whom, when and where, and always who was going to pay for it. It was twenty-seven months of hell. Chet said I looked like roadkill when I came home from those meetings.

It finally dawned on me that we needed to define the rights and responsibilities of METRO as well as the cities and counties. That also answered my six nagging "w" questions.

Of course, that led to yet another committee. As chair, my job was to get twenty-four cities and three counties to consider joining a regional planning process with roles, rights, and responsibilities clarified.

The tension crackling through the room at our first public meeting was palpable. There were handcuffs for the "METRO Police" and angry arguments against working together as a region. At the next meeting I presented the most outraged opponents with T-shirts that read, "I'm the Meanest Son of a Bitch in the Valley." We had a good laugh, clarified the five "w'" questions and eventually agreed on goals and objectives.

There was no model for a partnership of governments of this scale anywhere in the world. We had to figure it out ourselves. I met with the various groups who would be affected to better understand their fears and concerns and we gradually developed an outline of what the Grand Experiment might look like.

A study group provided an independent source of information that built trust, reassured local governments, and gave them confidence to support the Grand Experiment partnership with METRO, but only if METRO's authority was limited to dealing with issues of regional significance, and if cities and counties were true partners. No top-down planning allowed!! Although theoretical pie-in-the-sky planning may look good on paper it fails at the neighborhood level.

One of the most important changes was the formation of a Metropolitan Policy Advisory Committee (MPAC) of city, county, and special district officials, and a citizen representative from each county. It was quite controversial because it was widely believed by the "good government" folks that this committee would be a roadblock to success.

They were all wrong and MPAC has been instrumental in bringing consensus to what could have been a battlefield of growth management issues. Rena Cusma, METRO Executive Officer wrote after a successful process to plan for fifty years of growth, "The Metropolitan Policy Advisory Committee has been a vital partner in the process...."

Local governments gave up some autonomy, but gained a forum to resolve issues of metropolitan significance that would have been impossible to deal with individually. It helped significantly when METRO developed first class information and mapping systems that helped local government officials understand how truly connected the region was and how beneficial it would be to work together.

The end result of the successful Grand Experiment called METRO is that local governments understand they are better off with it—than without it. The question is will it prevent back-to-back malls and freeways from replacing farm and forestland? It is our strong belief that the answer is yes.

I've talked with people from Colorado, New Mexico, Texas, the Carolinas, and as far away as Tanzania about the METRO Grand Experiment but so far it is unique to the Portland metropolitan area.

Helping gain consensus about the value of regional planning was about listening to people's concerns and ideas, and how to evaluate, organize and present accurate information and stay on point—all things I learned from my Henley High School speech and debate teacher. However, if there are hidden agendas being effective irritates people to say the least.

Hidden agendas drove the Oregon Department of Land Conservation and Development (DLCD) staff to oppose my appointment to the Land Conservation and Development Commission (LCDC).

I suspect their opposition was based on at least three issues: 1) They thought I would not be quiet about an occasional quiet misinterpretation of State law if they wanted to skew a decision, 2) I played a major role in increasing METRO's regional land use authority, and 3) They saw METRO's increased authority as a threat to their State department. Their expectations of me were correct. I was trouble waiting to happen.

It probably didn't help that I was only the seventh woman appointed in the twenty-two year history of LCDC, and the only woman on the Commission. That was the tradition except for a four-year period between 1999 and 2004 when three of the seven Commissioners were women. Only Governor John Kitzhaber broke with tradition when he appointed Mayor Lindsay Berryman, Nancy Leonard, and me to LCDC and the world did not end.

The Senate confirmation of my appointment was debated for what seemed like forever. Dick Townsend, League of Oregon Cities Director put it this way: "Just a note of congratulations on your 17-9 success in the Senate. It is nice to have someone say 'no way' and then prevail. I admire your strength of conviction." I had refused to rebuke Oregon's statewide land use planning laws in the three-hour long grilling I got from the Rules Committee hearing prior to the Senate's debate and vote. That was another First Step challenge victory.

Just as my "you ask too many questions" City Manager had done, the DLCD bureaucracy tried to marginalize me and get rid of me. I'm a stickler for following the law and not making it up as you go. They, on the other hand, had elevated land-use planning from a development tool to a religion and they were the priests in charge of the program. Some of us call them the True Believers.

I caught them with their marginalizing strategy pants at half-mast at my second meeting. I sensed that Chair Bill Blosser wondered about some of my questions during my first meeting. So at the second meeting, I tracked what others were saying and how it fit with the material in my notebook before I said anything.

I quickly realized something was awry so I quietly asked Commissioner Randy Franke who was sitting next to me if I could look at his notebook. His material was different than mine. It was no an accident that I had only the working drafts of every business item for our two-day meeting instead of the final draft. What else could it be except an attempt to make me look unprepared and foolish?

The True Believers didn't know I could smell deceit a mile away and they also didn't know I was dedicated to dealing with secrets out in the open. I interrupted the meeting respectfully, "Mr. Chair. There has been a mistake. The staff reports in my notebook are different than those in Commissioner Franke's notebook. Would you ask staff to give me the correct information?" One of the True Believers had to give me his notebook. They never tried that again.

Their hidden agenda and sabotage attempt was confirmed when I discovered later that same day that I was the only new commissioner that wasn't given business cards. I told the woman in charge of such things, "The staff were so sure they were going to marginalize me and get rid of me they told you to hold off printing them." She looked down at the floor, her face turned red, and she said I would have them at the next meeting. She kept her word.

A frightening fact about bureaucracies is that staff controls the information and they can control the outcome by giving elected officials just what you need to know, to do exactly what they want you to do. Most bureaucrats are not so devious, but the taxpayers who pay their bills and elected officials need to be alert and do their homework.

I discovered that this same State land use department, the one that forced every city and county in the state to have a Citizen Involvement Program—didn't have one and what's more didn't want one. The Commission agreed that it was more than a little hypocritical and voted to force the department to have rules to include citizens in its planning process. With stalling tactics bordering on sabotage it took four years, but a Citizen Involvement Program for the state was finally approved.

As my first term ended, I learned Governor Kitzhaber was not going to reappoint me. Two groups were lobbying against me: the DLCD staff, of course, and 1000 Friends of Oregon, a land use watch-dog organization that supported my first appointment but was disappointed that I was not in lock step with them.

For example, at more than a few meetings one of their members or staff would either show pictures of big farmhouses or complain about them. Finally, I confronted them, "Are you saying you want this Commission to limit the amount of money a farmer can spend on his or her house?" "Oh, no," was the answer but it was clear that was exactly what they wanted to make it easier for young farmers to buy property. While that may be a worthy goal, the amount of money a farmer wants to spend on either a small house or a big house should not be the business of the State of Oregon. That view made me enemy #1.

I had been a long time supporter of 1000 Friends and was dismayed that their original mission seemed to have been compromised. They confirmed my suspicions during committee meetings that I chaired to finally define the difference between rural and urban lot sizes as the Supreme Court had ordered the Commission to do twenty years earlier:. It affected less than 1% of the land mass in the State.

The 1000 Friends of Oregon representative would vote in favor of committee findings and proposals and then cancel their vote at the following meeting. The reason for their peculiar actions became clear after the Commission approved our committee proposals. I received a flyer warning me that the sky was falling. The Commission supported the zoning that had been in place for twenty-five years and did not increase minimum lot sizes to build a home from two acres to ten acres as preferred by the True Believers and 1000 Friends.

It was obvious that 1000 Friends of Oregon no longer worked toward solutions because solutions couldn't be sold as fundraiser scare tactics. I didn't want to continue to support an organization that I saw as dishonest and deceitful. So I called my attorney to change my will. 1000 Friends of Oregon would no longer receive the proceeds from my IRA after my death.

The Oregon Home Builders Association (OHBA) and its formidable lobbyist, Jon Chandler, had opposed my first appointment to LCDC but rallied on my behalf for a second term of office. Governor Kitzhaber relented. He reappointed me.

I thought I knew why 1000 Friends and the OHBA had flip-flopped on my appointment. My hunch was that both groups thought I would try to impose a Portland metropolitan area land-use plan statewide as a member of the State planning group, and that neither group understood that I steadfastly opposed top-down planning. I asked Jon if my hunch was correct.

He laughed, "No. I told the Governor, "She used to be my pain in the ass. Now she's your pain in the ass, and any list that goes forward without her name on it is dead on arrival." My name was on the list sent to the State Senate for confirmation and I was reappointed over the dead bodies of the DLCD staff and 1000 Friends of Oregon.

I finally had an ally when Mayor Lindsay Berryman from Southern Oregon joined the Commission. We were called the "Nurses Mafia" because we had been nurses and we believed the program was going to lose the support of voters if some of the rules for rural areas were not changed. There were also rules that conflicted with each other and needed to be changed.

A new director, Paul Curcio, had ideas for streamlining the lengthy and overly complicated process and drew fire from the True Believers, 1000 Friends and Governor Ted Kulongoski, newly elected in 2002.

Two Commissioners sided with the Governor and began a quiet behind the scenes one-on-one lobbying campaign to have one of them takeover the directors position.

It was a legal train wreck waiting to happen, so I worked with our staff in the State Attorney General's office to write a position paper objecting to their antics, which put us in a dangerous legal position. Our attorney approved every word I wrote, and every word I read from my script in open session as well as a closed executive session. There were four attorneys at that meeting to protect the State's interest. It was just another secret deal that needed to be brought out into the open.

Of course, I was made out to be the bad guy. Mr. Curcio could see the handwriting on the wall with the Governor's strong opposition and resigned. The Governor then met with the department managers and three Commissioners including me. Instead of thanking me for preventing a costly court suit, the Governor dissed me, "You need to learn to get along." He denied that in a discussion with me when he was running for Governor that he had said there were problems with the statewide program. He has made the very same statements in public since that denial.

So I gave up on the Governor.

It must have been difficult for Governor Kulongoski to transition from serving as Oregon Attorney General and the Supreme Court. In both positions he interpreted and had the power to change laws that didn't seem to work anymore. Instead of over-riding State laws that he didn't like regarding the duties and obligations of Commissioners, he should have convinced the Legislature to change the Statutes. Instead, he violated State Statutes regarding Land Conservation and Development commissioners and their authority and obligation to hire and fire the Director of the Department. Governors could and should try to influence the process, but they should honor the State laws that clearly say that Governors do not make the final decision.

Wouldn't you think a $3,000 campaign contribution would at least have gotten me a phone call to find out my side of the story? The Governor was rude and crude, his statements were out of line, and he was dead wrong. He had been co-opted by the two Commissioners. The True Believers sent a statewide email to planners celebrating my come-uppance.

You define yourself by your enemies as well as your friends. I consider it an honor to be on the Hit List of the True Believers and Governor Ted Kulongoski. Kulongoski's professional relationships are one way—you help him. For example, he recruited Nan Evans to be the new director. She had cleaned up the coastal program and stopped the illegal use of federal money. She did a fine job as director, but the Governor decided he wanted a "figure head" to represent the department. He expected Nan to demote herself to deputy director, continue to do the work of the director, but for less money. She gave up on the Governor, too, and went to work for the Nature Conservancy.

Mayor Berryman tried to discuss the need for change with Governor Kulongoski when she was taking him on a tour of her city in his limousine. The Governor "dissed" her saying basically that everything was fine and to forget it. Mayor Berryman resigned seeing no light at the end of that tunnel.

For five years, I said, "If the Commission doesn't make some changes, the program will sink of its own weight and it will lose public support." The True Believers would roll their eyes, "There she goes again."

The Governor and the True Believers have been completely co-opted by 1000 Friends of Oregon, or as some now say 1000 Enemies of Oregon, and were an integral part of voters finally getting fed up and saying, "NO" to the bureaucrats beloved land use plan, which they treated as if it had come down from a mountaintop written in stone never to be changed. It did indeed "sink of its own weight" just as Commissioner Lindsay and I predicted. The True Believers and 100 Friends of Oregon were wrong about change being unnecessary.

I suspect that Governor Tom McCall, father of Oregon's first land use plan, would have thought that over the years as "Senate Bill 100" played out in the real world, that it might need to be tweaked, and he is likely spinning in his grave at the self righteousness and stubbornness of those land use idols who followed him.

Governor Neil Goldschmidt appointed me to the first Oregon Progress Board because I called his friend, Chairman and CEO Roger Breezley of U. S. Bancorp to pitch Gresham as a good place to build the bank's new Operation Center. I was one of three women on the committee that was chaired by the Governor.

Governor Goldschmidt had the courage to propose that State government should be accountable. Oregon was the first state to have measurable benchmarks to evaluate the quality of government services.

Money was not spent on legislators "take home projects" unless they met the Benchmarks to implement the State Strategic Vision for quality jobs, safe, caring and engaged communities, and healthy sustainable surroundings. Oregon prospered under Governor Goldschmidt's leadership.

Governor Barbara Roberts championed her predecessor's drive for government accountability. The Progress Board, chaired by the Governor, won a national award for the Oregon Benchmarks, which caught the attention of Vice President Al Gore. As the Vice Chair of the Progress Board, I accompanied the Governor and her staff to Washington, D.C. to receive the award, and meet with the Vice President. He also took us on a tour of his office, the Eisenhower Executive Office Building, and arranged for a photographer to record our meeting—a photograph that I treasure to this day.

The current Progress Board gives its report every year on whether the State is meeting the Benchmarks. The excitement and sizzle is gone. Now it's good but old news that State leaders still believe in Governor Goldschmidt's vision of a State government that is accountable to the people.

Back in my small city that had welcomed almost 40,000 new people since they elected me Mayor, I was astonished to receive the Citizen of the Year Award. An editorial in The Outlook justified giving the award for the first time ever to an elected official: "The selection is a controversial one, but after it's all said and done, what McRobert has done for this city over the last nine years is unparalleled by most volunteers. That's right, the Gresham mayor is an unpaid position."

As the new millennium ended I was astounded to be chosen as one of the "Eighteen Most Influential People in East Multnomah County History." *The Outlook,* "which had argued, agreed, haggled, and harassed her on different occasions," acknowledged "McRobert had redefined the role of mayor in the City of Gresham and exhibited badly needed energy and leadership. Her guiding principle was to ask herself on each issue, "Will it matter in twenty years?"

The unsolicited complimentary letters I received when I retired from City Hall were surprising. I have to admit I was pleased because the writers had nothing to gain politically since I would soon be history. My favorite was the one written by John and Sue Andersen, "There once was a mayor named Gussie. Who some people thought was too fussy. But after ten years of her vision and energy, we now see that Gresham is the envy of many!" John was a key partner in our effort to get twenty-four cities and three counties to work with Metro. So was Ethan Seltzer who wrote, "None of what we accomplished could have happened without you. Your ability to see connections and possibilities moved things forward at crucial points. I am particularly in awe of your willingness to put yourself out there, take a stand, and take risks. Rest assured, you have made a substantial difference." What a difference a couple of decades made in expanding expectations and opportunities for women.

1. The campaign begins. 2. Victory for Jade and Gussie. 3. Officially Her Honor. 4. Old City Hall. 5. New City Hall. 6. Mbari Arts and Cultural Center.

1. Gussie with Nigerian women. 2. Chief MKO Abiola. 3. Mrs. Alhaja Kuridat Abiola. 4. First Oregon Progress Board chaired by Governor Neil Goldschmidt. 5. Governor Roberts entourage meeting with Vice President Al Gore. 6. LCDC members .7. Chet, Gussie, Senator Mark Hatfield at Hatfield's retirement dinner.

214

City of Gresham Mayor Gussie McRobert

1988-1998

1. West Side Rail Opening, Commissioners Earl Blumenauer, Beverly Stein and Gussie.
2. Composite of my ten years as Mayor.

A nimals were an important part of our family's healing process. They taught us valuable lessons. Animals let you know when they want love and attention—they don't play gotcha games and make you guess when they want to be petted and stroked, and then punish you if you don't get it right. Over our thirty-eight years, we had two dogs and ten cats.

At the Wallula house, there were squirrels galore. You could set your clock by their twice-daily arrivals, scurrying down the fence, hopping over to a pine tree, and scrambling down to the deck. Squirrels are rare at our Persimmon house because the coyotes, raccoons, and opossums keep the population low. Only three squirrels come to eat and drink filtered water. I call them Herbie, Helen, and Herbie Junior.

The first time Herbie investigated the people in the new house, he found a covered flat bird feeder nailed to the deck railing. He ate for an hour and a half and slept for three hours. He's been coming two times a day ever since. He brought a friend and then they announced a baby, Herbie Junior. Herbie always dances on the deck railing and chatters until I acknowledge their presence. The one time I did not get walnuts and peanuts added to their regular feed, he stood very still on the railing, looked me straight in the eye, and scolded me soundly. I got the message and he hasn't had to chew me out since.

When I took the flat feeder off of the railing and hung it from a beam, he jumped with ease to claim it as his. But, he grew bored with that routine and I gave the feeder to the Goodwill. Three years later, Herbie decided he wanted to resume his naps suspended in the air. He let me know that I had fouled up by climbing to the top of a triangular trellis and squawking and looking up where his airborne bed had been. If I told you how much I spent to replace that particular version of feeder, you would likely think I was a little squirrelly. But Herbie and his family are happy and it is a safe place to sleep, far above the reach of the coyotes, possums, and raccoons.

Skip picked enough strawberries to buy Flash, a Basset Hound. She settled into the new house until a carpenter hired to add a bedroom began tearing out walls. She took off on a run and unfortunately ran in front of a car and was killed. She loved to lick empty ice cream cartons and she would always get her head stuck and then howl to be rescued. She was a clown and a joy.

Jastka, a name suggested by Chet because it included an initial from each of our names, was a beautiful German Shepherd that had to be taken back to the kennel to get barking lessons. The guys liked to sleep on top of the swimming pool cover in the summertime. They called it "covering." Jastka thought it looked like fun and barked her approval.

Marc told her "No" because he was afraid she would disturb the neighbors so she stopped barking altogether. Fortunately, she recovered her voice with only one lesson. Jastka would bark the first time somebody came to our house. After that initial visit, she knew who was at the door before it was opened and didn't bark again.

Jade, our second and beloved German Shepherd, barked each and every time anyone rang the doorbell and then stood between us and whoever had come to visit until we assured her they were OK. She made editorial comments about television newscasts. She got that from me. I groan in disgust—like give me a break—when it seems as though a news story isn't on the up and up. Everyone said she sounded just like me. She was a love.

We had nine cats: one pure-white angora, three orange tabbies, two Manx show-offs, one calico, one midnight black, and one tuxedo black and white. All beauties! Tropical fish entertained the cats.

Snow Ball was the resident cat at the McRobert household when we combined our two families. She was the only cat I've ever known who liked to ride in the car. She made it clear that she wanted to help me with grocery shopping. She sat on my shoulder while I drove us to the store and retreated to the back seat when the car stopped. Snow Ball was not a happy camper if I didn't plan my shopping to coincide with the cool part of the day so she could go with me.

Tiger One came with us to Chet's Wallula house. He was the resident physician. When he slept, not on the couch, but on someone's bed we knew that some kind of health problem would soon follow. He was never wrong and he didn't leave a sick bed except to eat and use the litter box until whoever was ailing was well. Tiger One frustrated the neighborhood dogs. If they tried to chase him, he would sit down and stare down the critter that wanted him to run.

Maverick and Mustang, our Manx wonders, were the only cats that didn't just show up and move in. We actually bought them. They could jump from the floor to the top of our kitchen cupboards with ease. The Christmas tree had to be anchored on all sides with nylon fishing line because Maverick thought it was great fun to climb to the top and streak down to the floor.

Mustang was the victim of a veterinarian's bungled neutering surgery and hormonal treatment didn't help. He was miserable and finally we couldn't stand to see him suffer any longer. Losing good friends is hard.

Maverick then claimed Chet as his personal property. If I sat next to Chet, he would push his way in between us. He would have nothing to do with me until most of the guys were grown and gone and he realized he might have to rely on me to get fed. Suddenly, I was his best buddy.

Maverick waited eagerly for the first freeze. Then the berries on our neighbor's Mountain Ash tree would ferment and birds came from everywhere to party. The drunken birds would attempt to fly through the closer of two triangular shaped windows at either end of our living room's vaulted ceiling. They were certain it was a flyway. We taped kites to the window in hope they would turn, but it didn't work. Maverick would wait patiently on the flat roof next to the window knowing that the drunkards would be stunned and easy picking after they hit the glass. He was a happy but lazy hunter!

Jasmine was a calico sweetheart that wandered into a house where Tim was living with some friends because they slept with the door open. When he went off to school, she came to live with us. Jasmine was a spook. The only time she was friendly was when she could sleep on my desk under what she thought was her heat lamp. The only other time Jasmine admitted that she liked living with us was when the windows had to be left open in mid-winter until a malfunctioning furnace could be repaired. She wanted to come and go without the indignity of having to ask humans to open a door for her.

Midnight was of course a black cat. She would have rung the doorbell if she could have reached it and said, " I've decided to honor you with my presence." She used to sleep on Chet's shoulder when he was watching television. After about a year, Chet found her lying lifeless in the driveway. Our veterinarian couldn't tell us why she died. She was a joy the short time she was with us.

Tiger Two scratched and meowed loud enough that we finally heard him trapped underneath the hot tub in our bathroom. We rescued him and he stayed for nine years. Tiger Two let us know he was in charge.

I bought an electric kitty litter box. When he discovered that the litter rake moved when he stepped into the box he started dancing in and out to make his new toy purr. Then he looked for ways to stymie the rake. He peed on the metal that supported the rake as it moved back and forth and then kicked litter on it. His plan worked. The rake couldn't get past the gummed up litter mess, which meant I had to take it apart and wash it. The third time he stopped the rake in its tracks I told him, "OK, you win. It's out of here."

In his later years with us, Tiger Two apparently reached a peace agreement with the birds and squirrels that came to visit. He never made a move to harm any of them and enjoyed their acrobatic shows as much as we did.

Tiger Two made it perfectly clear that he wanted our house to be a one-cat house after I made the mistake of befriending a stray female calico. It was almost a battle to the death, his death, so I had to find Callie a new home.

Tiger Two made the move with us to our downsized house and immediately made friends with neighbors. He loved sleeping in the sun and watching and waiting for golf carts. They fascinated him.

Tiger Two made me see cats differently. I stayed up until 1:00 AM to let him in because the only kitty door we had led to an unheated garage and there was a raging winter storm blowing outside.

The next night, I told him if he didn't come back by 11:00 PM he would be sleeping in the cold garage. At exactly 11:00 PM, Tiger Two was at the door asking to come inside. I thought what is this? So the next night I told him to be back by 10:00 and the night after that 10:30. Then for the next two nights I tried

9:00 and 9:30. He was back on time--every time. I had no choice except to look at cats in a whole new light. Tiger Two was a love and we felt blessed that he chose to live with us. We took a chain saw to the malfunctioning hot tub that trapped him but brought him into our lives.

Just before Chet died, we received a call from a woman who rescues abandoned animals offering us an orange tabby cat that needed a home as winter approached. Remembering the lesson I learned from Tiger Two that cats were not to be treated as stuffed toys, I told her we would gladly welcome him but I wanted Morgine Jurdan, an animal communicator to check in with him to ask what name he wanted to be called.

It was a Friday night, and Morgine recommended that we give him the weekend to check us out to see if he wanted to live with us, and she also said he didn't care for the name I was thinking of: Mufasa, King of the Pride from the Lion King. He preferred to be called Alexander and pointed out that it could be shortened to Alex and he wanted to know how I would shorten Mufasa? So we settled on Alexander and Alex. I know when it's best to fold. You never win an argument with a cat.

On Monday morning, Morgine checked in with him about his weekend with us, and asked him whether he wanted to adopt us. We were pleased to learn we had passed his test! He also wanted us to know he liked sleeping on a bed and his purpose was to bring joy to his humans. I thought OK being just a tiny bit skeptical.

Alex seemed more than a little skeptical about completely trusting humans again after being abandoned. He wanted out on the deck every five minutes as a way to get attention and affection, and he wouldn't sit on anyone's lap more than a few seconds. Alex learned to trust us and he is an absolute joy rightfully expecting to be adored.

He visits my neighbors on his walkabouts and especially enjoys their son, Jason, who is heroically recovering from a brutal attack by a Waste Management garbage truck that hit his car while he was stopped waiting for a red traffic light to turn green in San Diego. Alex might be our third orange tabby medical practitioner.

Trevor, a beautiful black and white tuxedo cat, was a feral outdoor cat for fifteen months, which a few people now dispute because he is so calm, loving, and trusting. He came to our door soon after we moved to our new downsized house but with my husband dying, my Tiger cat dying, and having a house full of boxes that needed to be unpacked, I just wasn't up to taking on a new cat. And Tiger Two had made it clear that he wanted us to be a one-cat household. But I always put out food and water for him in the morning and afternoon, and after my experience with Alex, I had Morgine Jurdan check in with him.

Morgine reported that we had a choice of calling him either Trevor or Rooster. We chose Trevor, which suited his symphony-conductor-in-a-tuxedo look. She said he feared being trapped and she told me to visualize messages to him about how he could enter and leave our house. I wasn't so overwhelmed that I couldn't at least do that. I let him know that he could come in the front door, go straight down the stairs, and out the sliding glass door downstairs in our daylight basement.

Trevor finally trusted me enough to let me pet him and then pick him up in my arms. Then I learned about Tellington Touch or TTouch, a massage technique discovered by a Florida veterinarian, Dr. Linda Tellington-Jones. When I did an Internet search for TTouch, I found to my surprise that a former neighbor, Judy Boyd, was a practitioner. Since Trevor didn't come at specific times of day, Judy couldn't treat him but she taught me how to do TTouch.

I held Trevor and petted and stroked him as Judy showed me for as long as he wanted to be loved. That was usually two hours in the morning and two hours in the afternoon. I was still in shock from Chet's death and we helped each other heal. Gradually his trust grew and his fear diminished so he finally felt safe enough to be inside with the door closed.

On September 25th, fifteen months after Trevor first looked into our house, when the nights were beginning to chill I think he remembered the previous winter with temperatures down to nineteen degrees and 30 miles an hour wind howling through the trees.

Alex alerted me that something was going on at the front door. It was Trevor. He flew through the door when I opened it, streaked down the stairs, and waited for me to open the sliding glass door just as I had tried to show him visually for many months.

We went through the same routine the next night, but on the third night he stayed inside. He slept downstairs and he stayed downstairs during the day. Alex wasn't too sure about this interloper and showed his displeasure by staying out until 11:00 PM. That was a big mistake. Trevor came upstairs and he's been an upstairs cat to this day. They are best buddies now.

But Trevor the Terrific had nightmares and he cried out in his sleep. I know at least one golfer yelled at him and chased him off the fairway because I screamed at him to "Stop that. Don't you ever do that again!" I held Trevor, petted him, loved him, reassured him that he was safe and that nobody was going to hurt him ever again. Gradually the bad dreams stopped. Trevor is my hero and protector. No matter where he is in the house, he always faces the door and growls like a dog at any suspicious sound.

I tried the be-back-by-a-time-certain routine on Alexander the Greatest and Trevor the Terrific. They go for walkabouts and they come home on time. I suspect they also probably want to please someone who has provided a stable home for them when they've been on their own and know how difficult that can be. The treats they know they'll find in their bowls undoubtedly encourage them to keep track of the time.

We helped each other heal! there is no question about that. Alex is my lap cat, and Trevor is my watch cat.

Cats rule in this house with two exceptions. First, is when they invite an opossum to come in their house and spend the night. Trevor and Alex like to perch on the upper deck railing at night to watch the critters coming and going in our yard and on the golf course. When I opened the door to let them in for the night, an opossum was right behind them expecting to come inside. Fortunately, I was able to close the door before he made it inside. I draw the line at pet opossums or raccoons or coyotes.

The second exception is when a bird inadvertently comes inside through an open deck door and can't find the way back outside. That actually happened with a goldfinch, and Alex and Trevor had to stay in the bedroom with the door closed to give it a chance to find the way out.

After a time there was no chirping and no fluttering of wings so I let them out and soon heard a crash. Trevor was about to have a goldfinch snack over by a window that the tiny bird apparently had hoped was open.

I opened the window but the goldfinch didn't move toward it. I slowly cupped my hands around its tiny body and lifted it over the windowsill to the outside where I unfolded my hands providing the tiny beauty a platform to fly to safety. It was a wondrous experience and truly a blessing to have held a goldfinch in my hands ever so briefly. The goldfinches frequent my bird feeders and I wonder which one is the special one that trusted me enough to let me help it find its way home. I now have a black hawk taped on the sliding glass door so it doesn't happen again. Alex and Trevor will not have goldfinches for lunch in our living room.

Alexander the Greatest and Trevor the Terrific supervise my morning exercise routine in the basement. Without regular exercise, what I call "Aging Jock Syndrome" takes over and all the places that I mistreated playing football and high jumping and skiing complain.

Our routine starts with turning on the traffic light that I gave Chet for Christmas. Alex sits in front of it and let's me know he wants the lights on. Then he moves to a framed poster of a Porsche car with a license plate that reads McRobert. Porsche officials wanted Chet to sell their cars and had the poster made especially for him. He put it in his shop where I rescued it after we moved and had it framed. I don't know whether it's the car or his reflection in the glass that thrills Alex but he talks to the poster until I finish my routine. Trevor wondered what the excitement was about and joined Alex once but he wasn't impressed. He is on guard watching the door until we go up stairs. He is my protector. I am truly blessed.

There is no question in my mind that our animal friends helped our family heal and learn to trust life. Their unconditional love and devotion filled the holes in our hearts and our souls.

1. Flash. 2. Jastka. 3. Jade. 4. Tiger One. 5. Snow Ball. 6. Maverick and Mustang. 7. Maverick.
8. Midnight.

1. Tiger Two. 2. Jasmine. 3. Alexander the Beautiful. 4. Trevor the Terrific.

Chapter Twelve

Healing From
My Blackberry Winter

H ealing is subtle and doesn't happen in an instant or a month or a year. My experience has been that the encouragement of others, success at anything, building confidence, and counseling from friends, pastors, and professionals can help us heal. How do you know when you're healed? It's a continuous process. It doesn't come in a box. But you'll know it when you see it and feel it.

I certainly cannot compare myself to Margaret Mead but her Blackberry Winter theory about people learning from adversity rings true with me and I think it applies to me. I was eventually able to harvest the good things in life.

I can't speak for any one except myself. I believe you have to first and foremost survive mistreatment. Survival means getting through difficult times by putting one foot in front of the other, persevering, and believing in your worth as a human being, surviving while you wait for the right time to make changes.

Survival then creates hope that you will have a better life. With hope comes the ability to envision a better life, and take action toward it even in some comes the ability to envision a better life and take action. It may be accepting the situation, but changing your reaction. Or you can remove yourself from the problem situation and go onto something else. If you're apprehensive and fearful, are you certain your feelings are caused from something that is happening at the time of your response? Or is it one of your pesky "buttons" programmed years before like my "bad times follow good times" anxiety? You can peel those layers apart, one by one, until one day you have an Aha! Moment, and choose to shut off those buttons and tapes that were programmed to play over and over.

There is no formula. We must each find our own way. For me it was ending an abusive marriage, refusing to be a victim, counseling, finishing my education to become financially secure, attending Adult Children of Alcoholic Parents and Ala-Non Twelve Step meetings, being the only one to define my life, and being in a caring, supportive marriage with my best friend and the love of my life, Chet McRobert.

I've learned not to be afraid of change. Life flows like a river over rocky rapids and calm pools with little thought given to its beginning. What works for me when I have to face something new and challenging is to first be sure I understand its roots—the base facts. Then I move on to its purpose, possible consequences, and how it will be implemented to clarify the end game. And then go with the flow. I've found that you don't have to have all the answers before you take the plunge. If I had known the totality of most of the worthwhile things I've done in my life I wouldn't have had the courage to start. Including writing this book.

The first small step matters. The marvelous example I always use to explain this life scenario is the Deschutes River in Central Oregon. One sunny spring day our Gresham Get Away ski group stood at the top of Mt. Bachelor south of the City of Bend drinking in the beauty of the endless forests and the Three Sisters Mountains. It was our good fortune to be there on a day that a US

Forest Service guide was also standing at the top of the mountain talking with people about the geological history of the area.

He walked us over to a small *wet spot* hollowed out in the snow on the north side of the mountaintop. It was about a foot wide and was outlined by the volcanic soil beginning to reappear as the winter snow melted. He said the equivalent of "great things can come from small beginnings."

The ranger also said a small but powerful *wet spot* that appears every spring is the glacial beginning of the Deschutes River as the snow melts and makes its way down through the lava of Mt. Bachelor into the Little Lava Lake in the Cascade Mountains. Then it heads northeast past the Sunriver Resort and the City of Bend to irrigate the parched farmland in Central Oregon. Next it heads north to give river rafters a thrill and graciously accepts the flow of the many smaller streams in the Cascade Range as it continues north. Eventually its journey ends and the Deschutes River empties into the mighty Columbia River, and after traveling west past magnificent tree-covered cliffs, farms, towns, and cities, Mt. Bachelor's spring snow melting slowly, drop by drop, into one small insignificant *wet spot* at the top of the mountain becomes part of the Pacific Ocean. The first small step taken to overcome a difficult situation can lead to an unknown but quite wonderful adventure. Small steps matter!

Life is one adventure after another with one flowing into the next. I want my life to be as good as it can be. While I haven't always fit the norm for women of my era, I have always been true to myself just as Maude Melton taught me in the fifth grade: "To thy own self be true." I believe that wherever they are, my parents, my sister and brother, and my best friend and husband, Chet understand that I have indeed made it successfully from hell and back and I have done more than survive. I have thrived and I look forward to each new day.

I am grateful my mother did not subject me to the tyrannical control she experienced for too many years of her life so I had the freedom to roam unsupervised as a child in the Rocky Mountains of Montana and the green fields of southern Oregon. That freedom taught me it was good to have friends, that I could take care of myself, and explore new possibilities without fear. They were valuable lessons.

I am grateful to have lived in neighborhoods with playmates that were mostly boys. Authority figures, usually men, never daunted me, and although I was often the only woman at a meeting, I was always accepted as an equal.

I am grateful to have been taught that I have value as a woman. I am grateful for the positive legal changes affecting the role of women since my mother's enslavement and that women and men are now equal under the law. I appreciate and honor the work of the men and women who struggled and fought to make equality a reality.

I am grateful that if I had to be poor, it was in a country setting at a time when houses were not status symbols, and brands of clothing did not make or break you because the clothes worn by students from rich and poor families were the same.

I am grateful to have loved and lived with Chet McRobert in a partnership that worked for both of us. I am grateful for wonderful sons, a great daughter-in law, and granddaughters who are my pride and joy. I am grateful for all the animal friends that have blessed my life.

I am especially grateful that my country assertive woman roots went deep enough to survive the passivity that was expected of city women in the 1950s and 1960s.

I would like very much for all women to have options to do what they want to do personally and professionally even if it offends those who continue to be believe that women should "know their place." Life is about choices and not letting others define you by their beliefs. It doesn't help you and it doesn't help them.

I have come full circle with the troubled relationship with my mother. Both of our lives involved an awakening about ourselves that took us from falling to flying. To have gone from slavery to independence in fifty-six years is an amazing accomplishment. Her rage almost destroyed her as well as me, but we both got past those horrific times. She did not allow her dreams to be destroyed by her parents, grandparents, and the four brothers and sisters who abandoned her when she desperately needed their support.

My nephew, Murray Dean, showed me a letter written by Mother to her son, Dean, in 1941, just after Pearl Harbor. She asked if he was "going to join up" and added, "If I was a man, especially a young man, I think I would like flying, myself." I wish I had known about her wish to fly while she was alive. My husband, Chet, would have gladly taken her "flying" in his Beechcraft Bonanza airplane.

I don't long for the Saturday night dances of my youth. I enjoy writing and plan to do more of it with the help of my iMac. I do wish my antique stainless steel knee would stand up to skiing but my orthopedist says it won't. I enjoy the activities and goals of women helping women in two local organizations: the American Association of University Women and Soroptimist International of Gresham, and occasionally I email my Congressional delegation about women's issues brought to my attention by the National Organization of Women. I don't want to be in charge of anything. Been there. Done that. I don't long for the "good old days."

The "good old days" weren't so good for either women or men. But some politicians and their followers speak longingly about the "good old pioneer days" as the model for the perfect family. They don't mention that women were legally non-persons without basic rights as human beings and that men were expected to be tyrants.

During the year and a half that I spent writing this book, friends who I thought had happy childhoods have come forward with their stories. A three-year old girl dressed and put out on the streets of Azusa, California to fend for herself while her brother, the chosen one, was loved and cared for. Fortunately, neighbors took her into their home, and cared for her until she graduated from high school. This happened in the enlightened 1950s. Her mother told her that she was evil and the cause of a son's birth defect.

Another friend's grandmother had always been a bit too feisty to meet the expectations for women of her time. At age sixty, she wrote, "I can't take it any more." She committed suicide.

Another friend had the audacity to marry the man she loved instead of returning home to care for the family after graduating from college. After fifty years her mother still doesn't acknowledge the marriage and refuses to speak to her husband.

Children were property with no legal rights and that had consequences for boys as well as girls. A friend tells the story of his father being tortured by his parents. After his father finished the third grade, at age nine, his father told him he had to help at home and could no longer attend school. If his father disapproved of his work, he made him stand on a rock and then whipped him with a barbwire whip. His mother then had her turn. She preferred hitting him in the head with a cast iron frying pan. His sister said he was injured so badly they sometimes feared for his life. He escaped by joining the U.S. Army at age seventeen to fight in World War II. He carried more scars from the brutality of his parents than he did from the war.

I hope *FROM HELL & BACK: SURVIVE AND THRIVE* demonstrates that women and men have come a long way and that we must never allow others to take us back to the "good old days." We deserve better and so do the men in our lives. The rigid conformity that limited the opportunities of men and women has no place in the new millennium with satellites and space ships and freedom.

I want to end this particular journey with the kind words of Mike McKeever, who was such a help to local governments during the Metro process, and then moved on to the Sacramento Council of Governments: "As the first Chair of the Metro Policy Advisory Committee, a committee of twenty four cities and three counties authorized by the Metro Charter to advise the Metro Council on growth management and other issues there is no one who had a larger impact on the future of this region over the last several years than you. In an age when it seems that no one can get anything done, you always got things done. At a time when people don't know who they can believe, you always told the truth—even when no one wanted to hear it (especially when no one wanted to hear it). You always, always followed your conscience and values. You fought for what you believed in and woke up the next morning ready to work with people you had disagreed with the night before. You didn't hesitate to take a position, but also weren't too proud to reverse field when the facts called for it. What mattered to you was getting it right. Oregon is famous for producing political giants and you have a well-deserved place on that rare list. 'One of a kind' is one of the highest compliments

I can pay someone, and that is one of the first phrases that comes to mind when I think of your accomplishments."

What I learned growing up in Montana's Rocky Mountains and the farm country in Southern Oregon helped me find my way on the streets of Portland. I wouldn't change even one chapter of my soap opera life. I learned as much from the pain as I did from the pleasure.

I look forward to whatever is ahead. I know it will be interesting with some unexpected twists and turns. When all is said and done, I'm just a country girl who learned that when reasonable and open minded people sit down together, listen carefully to each others views, they can work toward an outcome that benefits everyone, and wonderful magical things can happen.

1. The jacket that helped Gussie overcome the "bad times always follow good times" syndrome.
2. Buddies forever: Alex and Trevor. 3. Deschutes River Basin map.

DeVoss & Augustus Family Genealogical Chart

Isaac DeVoss – Delia De Long

Ida Johnson - Mr. McMillan

Lester Augustus

Edward DeVoss – Carolyn Chilsun DeVoss

Della
Louise
Caroline
Doris
George & Walter
Leonard
Lloyd

Ida Johnson – Frank Augustus

Harold
Frank
Gladys
Elmer
Ethel
Guy

Elmer Augustus - Della Angia Augustus

Dean Edward
Marjory Yvonne

Harry Augustus -Anna Augustus

Doris Augustus Derthick

Dean Edward Augustus – Juanita Dahms

Murray Dean
Dennis Edward
Karl Douglas

Lester A Augustus – Iva Augustus

Dorothy Augustus Caulfield

Lester Augustus – Della DeVoss

Norma (Gussie) McRobert

Chester A McRobert, Jr. – Delores Kletzing

Marc Kelly*
Bradley Alan*

Marshall Brown, M.D. – Norma Augustus

Skip Rhody McRobert*
Gregory John Brown
Timothy Paul McRobert *

*Adopted by Gussie McRobert

*Adopted by Chester A (Chet) McRobert, Jr.

Chester A (Chet) McRobert, Jr. — Norma Jean (Gussie) McRobert

America's 159-Year History of Women's Rights

U.S. Constitution addressed the rights of generic "persons" and "citizens." The practical interpretation was that it only applied to men, and women and children were chattel—the property of men.

1848: First Women's Rights Convention in Seneca Falls, New York where Elizabeth Cady Stanton gives her "Declaration of Sentiments" speech listing eighteen areas of life where women were treated unjustly.

1920: Suffrage Act gave women the right to vote.

1925: The Suffrage Act was extended to Native American women and men.

1964: Title VII of the Civil Rights Act included a prohibition against employment discrimination on the basis of race, color, religion, national origin, or sex.

1965: The Supreme Court, in Griswold v Connecticut, overturned one of the last state laws prohibiting the prescription or use of contraceptives by married couples.

1971: The Supreme Court, in Reed v Reed, for the first time struck down a law treating men and women differently. The Court finally declares women as "persons," but uses a "reasonableness" test rather than making sex a "suspect classification," analogous to race, under the Fourteenth Amendment.

1972: The Supreme Court, in Eisenstadt v Baird, ruled that the right to privacy encompasses an unmarried person's right to use contraceptives.

1973: The Supreme Court, in Roe v Wade and Doe v Bolton, ruled that the Constitution protects women's right to terminate an early pregnancy, thus making abortion legal in the United States.

1974: The U.S. Congress passed the Equal Credit Opportunity Act giving women the right to credit making it possible for women to get financial loans without a male co-signer.

1981: U.S. Supreme Court, in Kirchberg v Feenstra, overturned the few remaining state laws designating a husband "Head and Master" with unilateral control of property owned jointly with their wives.

1996: The U.S. Supreme Court clarified the legal status of women by ruling unequivocally that women were equal to men under the law.

2004: U.S. Congress approved the Justice for All Act in 2004 mandating that rape evidence be tested for DNA.

2007: U.S. Supreme Court, in Ledbetter v Goodyear Tire and Rubber Company, Inc., ruled that employees' knowledge of pay discrimination is no longer the ruling factor in disputes. The Court set a 180-day timeline beginning from the date the discrimination actually occurred for filing complaints even if the employee had no knowledge of the discrimination until later.

Awards

Land Conservation and Development Commission, 2004

The Outlook: One of "Eighteen Most Influential People in East Multnomah County History," 2000

Matrix Award, Edith Knight Hill Award, for Improving Quality of Life, The Association for Women in Communications, Portland Chapter, 1999

Public Official of the Year, 1000 Friends of Oregon, 1998

ACT Leadership Award, Association of Commuter Transportation, 1998

Citizen of the Year, Gresham Area Chamber of Commerce and East Metro Association of Realtors, 1997

Mayor's Leadership Award, Oregon Mayor's Association, 1997

Distinguished Leadership Award for Elected Officials, American Planning Association, Oregon Chapter, 1996

Woman of the Year, Women's Transportation Seminar, Portland Chapter 1995

Woman of Distinction, Columbia River Girl Scout Council, 1992

Woman of Achievement, White Rose Award, March of Dimes, 1990

Women Helping Women, Soroptimist International of Gresham, 1988

Banner Award, Women in Communications, Inc., 1987

National Society of Association Executives, First Place for Radio Public Service Announcements for Oregon State Bar, 1987

Public Relations Society of America, First Place for Radio Public Service Announcements for Oregon State Bar, 1987

Associated Press Broadcast Award for Best Overall News Presentation in Metro, KKSN Brave News Radio, 1980

Associated Industries of Oregon Foundation, Honorable Mention for Business Reporting, 1979

Stuart Anderson Citizenship Award, Gresham Area Chamber of Commerce, 1977

Gussie (Norma J.) McRobert
PO Box 310, Gresham, OR 97030
H/B 503-665-4800 • Email: gmcrobert@comcast.net

Gussie (Norma J) McRobert was born in Colorado, spent her formative years in Montana and southern Oregon and has lived in Gresham, Oregon since 1955. Gussie was married to longtime Gresham businessman, Chet McRobert, for thirty-eight years before his death in 2003. They raised five sons and are blessed with three granddaughters. She is a former Registered Nurse with Bachelors and Masters Degrees in Communications, and an Associate Degree in Professional Nursing.

McRobert has twenty-five years of experience in broadcast journalism and public relations. She worked as a radio and television producer/reporter for Oregon Public Broadcasting where her reports were featured on National Public Radio's All Things Considered, Morning Edition, and Week End West; and news reports and documentaries for KKSN-AM Radio and news and public service features for KGW-AM Radio, covering city and county governments throughout the Tri-County area and Vancouver.

As owner of RX Communications, McRobert specialized in public service promotions for nonprofit organizations and government agencies. Her radio public service productions won local and national awards. Rx Communications—Gussie McRobert is now registered with the State of Oregon under the Independent Artists and Writers category. Rx Communications owns the registered website domain names of properwoman.net, fallingtoflying.com, theproperwomanthe tyrannyof expectations.com, and fromhellandbacksurviveandthrive.com.

McRobert's past public service includes:

> KBPS AM/FM Advisory Committee, Past President
>
> Private Industry Council, Economic Development Committee
>
> Multnomah County Planning Commission, Vice Chair
>
> Gresham Parks Commission, Chair, Vice Chair, Secretary
>
> Mayor, City of Gresham

McRobert's Public Service continued:

Metro Growth Management Policy Advisory Committee

Metro Policy Advisory Committee

Regional Governance Committee

Regional Water Supply Taskforce

Oregon Progress Board, Vice Chair

Livable Oregon, Inc., Past President

Oregon Mayors Association, Board of Directors

Gresham Progress Board, Chair

Gresham Area Prevention Partnership

Oregon Land Conservation and Development Commission

As mayor, McRobert initiated the city's first community-wide visioning program to guide transportation planning and growth management until the year 2020. While an advocate of growth and "smart development," McRobert also initiated the first voter approved, open space rescue and trail development program in the state; which has preserved some 700 acres of buttes, watersheds, wetlands, and creek corridors, and also provide 55 miles of off-road trails for recreation. She championed citizen involvement and greatly expanded the opportunities for people to be involved in city government.

McRobert's personal commitment to herself to always "say it like it is" sometimes provoked other regional leaders, but was consistent with her vow to always honor her values and conscience -- even if no one wanted to hear it.

Source Attributions

INTRODUCTION:

1. About Women's History: Abigail Adams Quotes.

2. Answers.com: women's rights, dates of major change and English Common Law.

3. Wikipedia: Abigail Adams. "Quotes by John Adams:" John Adams.

4. A Timeline of Women's Legal History in the United States and Georgetown University: Quotes of Abigail and John Adams.

5. Parents, Partners, and Personal Jurisdiction:, Rhonda Wasserman, 1995. Examples of how women's lives were affected by lack of specificity about women's rights in the Constitution and Bill of Rights.

6. The Constitution of the United States.

7. Wikipedia: Articles Of Confederation.

8. Legal Information Institute: Bill of Rights, Amendment V.

9. Wikipedia: "Head and Master" Laws.

10. Merriam Webster's Collegiate Dictionary 10th Edition: Definitions of slave, slavery, and slavey.

11. National Women's History Project: Timeline of Legal History of Women in the United States.

12. About Women's History: Married Women's Property Act: 1848, New York State.

13. About FindLaw: U.S. Supreme Court, REED V. REED, 404 U.S. 71 (1971)

CHAPTER ONE: FROM FALLING TO FLYING—NO ACCIDENTAL DEATH

1. Renaissance Center: Marriott at Renaissance Center Website. Detroit, MI.

2. Joseph Bizen, retired Ford Northwest Regional Manager confirmed event Chet and Gussie attended in Detroit 1978 was Ford Motor Company's 75th Anniversary Celebration.

3. Yale National Initiative Website: Infanticide and Abortion.

4 Yale-New Haven Teachers Institute Website: Curriculum Unit 82.06.03: Kathleen London, The History of Birth Control.

5. Cesarean Voice Website: Babies are Conscious: David Chamberlain, PhD.

6. Consciousness in Infants: Colwyn Trevarthen and Vasudevi Reddy.

7. Colyn Trevarthen and Dr. Vasudevi Reddy: education and work history.

8. The National Child Project: Newborn Life: Key Controversies in the Last Decade, David Chamberlain, PhD.

CHAPTER TWO: FAMILY SECRETS AND THE BLACK SHEEP

1. State of Kansas Website: Government, Facts and Symbols: Women's Legal Rights in Kansas Constitution.

2. Marshall County Kansas Website: Welcome and map of Kansas showing location in State.

3. Wikipedia: Comstock Law banned information about birth control.

4. LLI / Legal Information Institute: Supreme Court Collection, Griswold v. Connecticut, June 7, 1965 overturned Comstock Law.

5. Yale National Institute: History of Birth Control from 1840.

6. Thumbnail History of Kerosene Lanterns: D.A. Pearson.

7. Orville Berger: Ninety-three old Waterville, Kansas historian.

8. Waterville, Kansas Website: Explore Our Victorian Heritage.

9. Wikipedia and City Data.com: Waterville, Kansas statistics and demographics.

10. Cyclopedia of State History, Michael Delaney: One sentence: "Waterville then consisted of one portable house."

11. JSTOR: Equal Credit Opportunity Act approved by Congress in 1974.

12. Y! Secret Shopping/Scripophily.com: Basin Montana Tunnel Company 1934–1937.

13. Women's International Center: Women's History in America. PO Box 880736, San Diego, CA 92168.

14. U.S. Congress passed the Equal Credit Opportunity Act of 1974.

CHAPTER THREE: THE UNWANTED DAUGHTER

1. American Values Website: News Release: The Age of Unwed Mothers, 1999.

2. Common law marriages, Wikipedia.

3. Answers.com and Wikipedia: Dysfunctional Families

4. Y! Secret Shopping/Scripophily.com: Basin Montana Tunnel Company, 1934 to 1937.

5. Montana Legends: Merry Widow Health Mine in Basin.

6. Historical Development of Radio.

7. Henley High School booklets titled How to Apply for a Job. How Many Jobs.

CHAPTER FOUR: DEAN: THE FAVORED SON

1. Marriage and Seabees information provided by Murray Dean and Louise Augustus, son and daughter in law of Dean Edward Augustus.

CHAPTER FIVE: MARJORY: MY SISTER—MY SAVIOR

1. Westinghouse Electric Corporation, Sunnyvale, California website. Blair's Business College, Life Scholarship Certificate. Colorado Springs CO. 1935.

2. Google Earth map of Durant Avenue & Shattuck Avenue, Berkeley, California.

CHAPTER SIX: OFF TO THE BIG CITY

1. The National Center for Victims of Crimes: Incest.

2. Divorce decree No. 289 565, Circuit Court of the State of Oregon for the County of Multnomah Department of Domestic Relations.

3. Testimony of Registered Nurse Joyce Lakey regarding Dr. Marshall Brown's promiscuity.

4. Journal of the American Psychoanalytical Association: Freud and Feminine Subjectivity, Leon Hoffman, 1996.

5. Wikipedia: Domestic Violence.

CHAPTER SEVEN: SECRETS TO TRUTH—OUT OF THE DARKNESS

1. Women's International Center: Women's History in America, passive, cooperative, obedient role of women.

2. New York University Press, Law, Gender, & Injustice: A Legal History of U.S. Women, Joan Hoff, 1991, women serve as jurors, estate administrators, Congress passed civil rights laws that included women, 1964.

3. Women's History Project, Living the Legacy: women not issued credit cards "in their name" needed male co-signer or husband's permission, bank loans required male co-signer.

4. Places Where Women Made History, Women and Equal Rights: Women were to marry, do housework, raise a family. Could not control earnings, nor vote or defend themselves in court, inequities to women if divorced.

5. Federal Trade Commission, Equal Credit Opportunity, 1964.

6. FindLaw, U.S. Supreme Court, Reed v. Reed, 1971. The Court gave women the right to be executors of estates and were also given a classifications as "Persons" with legal rights.

7. Ingentaconnect: Gender roles as predictors of psychological health, masculine Model skews result.

8. Journal of Personality Assessment: Concurrent Validity of the MMPI-2 Feminine Gender Role (GF) is inconsistent.

9. A Jove Book published by arrangement with William Morrow & Company, *Hidden Malpractice, How American Medicine Mistreated Women.* Gena Corea, 1977. Male physicians devalued women, page 17.

10. A Jove Book published by arrangement with William Morrow & Company, *Hidden Malpractice, How American Medicine Mistreats Women,* Gena Corea, 1977. Pharmaceutical Advertisements In Medical Journals, page 94.

11. Planned Parenthood, Major U.S. Supreme Court Rulings on Reproductive Health and Rights (1965-2006).

CHAPTER EIGHT: THE LOVE OF MY LIFE.

1. Beech Aircraft Corporation, Wichita, Kansa, Beechcraft Musketeer single engine airplane, SPORT III, Model A23-19 OWNERS MANUAL.

2. Standard NO. 3 PILOT LOGBOOK, Gussie McRobert, September 1966.

CHAPTER NINE: WOMEN AT WORK.

1. Clark College Certificate of Proficiency in the field of Professional Nursing, Associate of Arts Degree, 1966.

2. Marylhurst Education Center, Bachelor of Arts Degree, Communications, 1979.

3. University of Portland Master of Arts Degree, Communications, 1981.

4. Oregon Business Magazine advertisement citing KKSN 91 AM RADIO, BRAVENEWS RADIO team winning top honors from Oregon Associated Press.

5. Norma J (Gussie) McRobert, KKSN-AM Radio Press Pass.

6. *The Oregonian* article, February 24, 1985: Oregon failed to act on three requests for sulfite warnings written by Gussie McRobert.

7. List of people who responded to Oregonian Public Notice ad about sulfite problems.

8. American Academy of Allergy Asthma & Immunology article "Sulfite Sensitivity" by Gaynor D. Govias, BSc.

9. Rx Radio News Network marketing material for public service announcements played on sixty Oregon stations.

10. Rx Radio News Network, Tune In To Health marketing material.

CHAPTER TEN: No Trickle Down Decisions

1. First Mayoral Term (2 years) began January 89 and ended December 1990.

2. Composite of City of Gresham Mayor Gussie McRobert, 1988-1998. Second Mayoral Term (4 years) began January 1991 and ended

December 1994. Third Mayoral Term (4) years) began January 1995 and ended December 1998.

3. Gresham Sister Cities: Records and websites of Owerri, Nigeria;, Sokcho City, Korea, Ebetsu City, Japan.

4. METRO Region 2040 Recommended Alternative Decision Kit, September 1944.

5. METRO Executive Rena Cusma, information about 2040 Growth Concept and value of committee of twenty-four cities and three counties working together.

CHAPTER TEN CONTINUED

6. Letter from Ethan Seltzer, Portland State University, December 18, 1998 regarding appointment to Land Conservation and Development Commission, 1996.

7. Department of Land Conservation and Development – List of women Commissioners from Director Lane Shetterley.

8. Letter from Richard C. Townsend, Executive Director Oregon League of Cities, 1996.

9. State of Oregon appointment to Land Conservation and Development Commission, 2000.

10. The Outlook Editorial about Gussie McRobert being awarded the 1997 Citizen of the Year Award.

11. *The Outlook* special edition of the Eighteen Most Important People In East Multnomah County History for the twentieth century.

12. Gresham Outlook article about being one of Eighteen Most Important People In East Multnomah County History for the Twentieth Century.

13. Poem received from John and Sue Andersen when Gussie McRobert retired and letter from Ethan Seltzer.

CHAPTER ELEVEN: Unconditional Love Heals

1. Dog Owner's Guide: The Tellington Touch.

CHAPTER TWELVE: HEALING FROM MY BLACKBERRY WINTER

1. Letter from Della Augustus to her son, Dean Augustus.

2. National Women's History Project: comments by Dr. Margaret Mead.

3. Deschutes River Conservancy.

4. Wikipedia-the Deschutes River.

5. Letter from Michael McKeever, McKeever/Morris, Inc. Portland, Oregon